Activities for the
Differentiated
Classroom

Gayle H. Gregory • Carolyn Chapman

CORWIN PRESS
Classroom

For information:

CORWIN PRESS

Corwin Press
A SAGE Publications Company
2455 Teller Road
Thousand Oaks, California 91320
CorwinPress.com

SAGE, Ltd.
1 Oliver's Yard
55 City Road
London EC1Y 1SP
United Kingdom

SAGE India Pvt. Ltd.
B 1/I 1 Mohan Cooperative
Industrial Area
Mathura Road, New Delhi
India 110 044

SAGE Asia-Pacific Pvt. Ltd.
33 Pekin Street #02-01
Far East Square
Singapore 048763

Printed in the United States of America.

ISBN 978-1-4129-5337-5

This book is printed on acid-free paper.

08 09 10 11 12 10 9 8 7 6 5 4 3 2 1

Executive Editor: Kathleen Hex
Managing Developmental Editor: Christine Hood
Editorial Assistant: Anne O'Dell
Developmental Writer: Jeanine Manfro
Developmental Editor: Colleen Kessler
Proofreader: Bette Darwin
Art Director: Anthony D. Paular
Cover Designer: Monique Hahn
Interior Production Artist: Scott Van Atta

Activities *for the* Differentiated Classroom

GRADE **1**

TABLE OF CONTENTS

Connections to Standards

This chart shows the national academic standards covered in each chapter.

MATHEMATICS	Standards are covered on pages
Numbers and Operations—Understand numbers, ways of representing numbers, relationships among numbers, and number systems.	9, 12, 23
Numbers and Operations—Understand meanings of operations and how they relate to one another.	17
Numbers and Operations—Compute fluently, and make reasonable estimates.	23
Algebra—Represent and analyze mathematical situations and structures using algebraic symbols.	20
Algebra—Use mathematical models to represent and understand quantitative relationships.	20
Geometry—Analyze characteristics and properties of two- and three-dimensional geometric shapes, and develop mathematical arguments about geometric relationships.	27
Communication—Use the language of mathematics to express mathematical ideas precisely.	27

SCIENCE	Standards are covered on pages
Physical Science—Understand properties of objects and materials.	31
Life Science—Understand characteristics of organisms.	39
Life Science—Understand organisms and environments.	34, 39
Earth Science—Understand changes in the earth and sky.	43, 45

SOCIAL STUDIES	Standards are covered on pages
Understand culture and cultural diversity.	55, 62
Understand the ways human beings view themselves in and over time.	62
Understand the interactions among people, places, and environments.	48, 52
Understand individual development and identity.	48
Understand how people organize for the production, distribution, and consumption of goods and services.	59

LANGUAGE ARTS	Standards are covered on pages
Read a wide range of print and nonprint texts to build an understanding of texts, of self, and of the cultures of the United States and the world; to acquire new information; to respond to the needs and demands of society and the workplace; and for personal fulfillment (includes fiction and nonfiction, classic, and contemporary works).	75
Apply a wide range of strategies to comprehend, interpret, evaluate, and appreciate texts. Draw on prior experience, interactions with other readers and writers, knowledge of word meaning and of other texts, word identification strategies, and understanding of textual features (e.g., sound-letter correspondence, sentence structure, context, graphics).	66, 71, 74, 75
Employ a wide range of strategies while writing, and use different writing process elements appropriately to communicate with different audiences for a variety of purposes.	78
Apply knowledge of language structure, language conventions (e.g., spelling and punctuation), media techniques, figurative language, and genre to create, critique, and discuss print and nonprint texts.	71, 81

Introduction

As a teacher who has adopted the differentiated philosophy, you design instruction to embrace the diversity of the unique students in your classroom and strategically select tools to build a classroom where all students can succeed. This requires careful planning and a very large toolkit! You must make decisions about what strategies and activities best meet the needs of the students in your classroom at that time. It is not a "one size fits all" approach.

When planning for differentiated instruction, include the steps described below. Refer to the planning model in *Differentiated Instructional Strategies: One Size Doesn't Fit All, Second Edition* (Gregory & Chapman, 2007) for more detailed information.

1. Establish standards, essential questions, and expectations for the lesson or unit.

2. Identify content, including facts, vocabulary, and essential skills.

3. Activate prior knowledge. Preassess students' levels of readiness for the learning and collect data on students' interests and attitudes about the topic.

4. Determine what students need to learn and how they will learn it. Plan various activities that complement the learning styles and readiness levels of all students in this particular class. Locate appropriate resources or materials for all levels of readiness.

5. Apply the strategies and adjust to meet students' varied needs.

6. Decide how you will assess students' knowledge. Consider providing choices for students to demonstrate what they know.

Differentiation does not mean always tiering every lesson for three levels of complexity or challenge. It *does* mean finding interesting, engaging, and appropriate ways to help students learn new concepts and skills. The practical activities in this book are designed to support your differentiated lesson plans. They are not prepackaged units but rather activities you can incorporate into your plan for meeting the unique needs of the students in your classroom right now. Use these activities as they fit into differentiated lessons or units you are planning. They might be used for total group lessons, to reinforce learning with individuals or small groups, to focus attention, to provide additional rehearsal opportunities, or to assess knowledge. Your differentiated toolkit should be brimming with engaging learning opportunities. Take out those tools and start building success for all your students!

Put It Into Practice

Differentiation is a Philosophy

For years teachers planned "the lesson" and taught it to all students, knowing that some will get it and some will not. Faced with NCLB and armed with brain research, we now know that this method of lesson planning will not reach the needs of all students. Every student learns differently. In order to leave no child behind, we must teach differently.

Differentiation is a philosophy that enables teachers to plan strategically in order to reach the needs of the diverse learners in the classroom and to help them meet the standards. Supporters of differentiation as a philosophy believe:

- All students have areas of strength.

- All students have areas that need to be strengthened.

- Each student's brain is as unique as a fingerprint.

- It is never too late to learn.

- When beginning a new topic, students bring their prior knowledge base and experience to the new learning.

- Emotions, feelings, and attitudes affect learning.

- All students can learn.

- Students learn in different ways at different times.

The Differentiated Classroom

A differentiated classroom is one in which the teacher responds to the unique needs of the students in that room, at that time. Differentiated instruction provides a variety of options to successfully reach targeted standards. It meets learners where they are and offers challenging, appropriate options for them to achieve success.

Differentiating Content By differentiating content the standards are met while the needs of the particular students being taught are considered. The teacher strategically selects the information to teach and the best resources with which to teach it using different genres, leveling materials, using a variety of instructional materials, and providing choice.

Differentiating Assessment Tools Most teachers already differentiate assessment during and after the learning. However, it is equally important to assess what knowledge or interests students bring to the learning formally or informally.

Assessing student knowledge prior to the learning experience helps the teacher find out:

- What standards, objectives, concepts, skills the students already understand

- What further instruction and opportunities for mastery are needed

- What areas of interests and feelings will influence the topic under study

- How to establish flexible groups—total, alone, partner, small group

Differentiating Performance Tasks In a differentiated classroom, the teacher provides various opportunities and choices for the students to show what they've learned. Students use their strengths to show what they know through a reflection activity, a portfolio, or an authentic task.

Differentiating Instructional Strategies When teachers vary instructional strategies and activities, more students learn content and meet standards. By targeting diverse intelligences and learning styles, teachers can develop learning activities that help students work in their areas of strength as well as areas that still need strengthening.

Some of these instructional strategies include:

- Graphic organizers

- Cubing

- Role-playing

- Centers

- Choice boards

- Adjustable assignments

- Projects

- Academic contracts

When planning, teachers in the differentiated classroom focus on the standards, but also adjust and redesign the learning activities, tailoring them to the needs of the unique learners in each classroom. Teachers also consider how the brain operates and strive to use research-based, best practices to maximize student learning. Through differentiation we give students the opportunity to learn to their full potential. A differentiated classroom engages students and facilitates learning so all learners can succeed!

CHAPTER 1

Mathematics

The Number Train

Standard
Numbers and Operations—Understand numbers, ways of representing numbers, relationships among numbers, and number systems.

Objective
Students will practice counting and writing numbers from 1 to 100.

Materials
Hundred Chart reproducible
empty soap boxes (10 per student)
scissors, construction paper, yarn, tape
small items such as straws, cotton swabs, or pennies (100 per student)

In this activity, students will use soap boxes to create a counting train. They will decorate each of ten train cars and count out sets of ten objects to fill each car. They can use the counting train to practice counting from 1 to 100 by ones and tens. By exploring the sequence of numbers, students will begin to understand the concept of place value.

1. To prepare for the activity, have students collect empty boxes from bars of soap. Each student will need ten boxes.

2. Help students cut out one long side from each of their ten soap boxes to make train cars. Then have them wrap the train cars with construction paper, leaving the top openings uncovered.

3. Next, help students poke holes in two opposite ends of each train car. Then have them tie the cars together with lengths of yarn.

4. Give students small items, such as straws, cotton swabs, or pennies, to put in each car. Help them count out sets of ten items for each car and label the cars *10, 20, 30,* and so on.

5. Once the cars are filled, have students practice counting the items from 1 to 100. Then let them practice skip-counting by tens, pointing to each car as they count.

◀ 6. Give students a copy of the **Hundred Chart reproducible (page 11)**. Have them write the numbers from 1 to 100 on the chart, using their train cars as a reference.

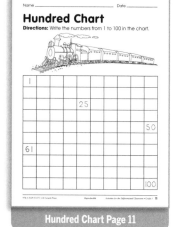

Hundred Chart Page 11

Ideas for More Differentiation

- Have high-degree mastery students combine sets of objects to practice addition skills, working with two-digit numbers.

- Have beginning mastery students make flashcards for each number from 1 to 100. Ask them to number 100 large index cards and attach the matching number of small stickers. Encourage them to place stickers in rows of ten for larger numbers.

Extend the Activity

- Have students bring collections of 100 items from home.

- Invite students to make paper chains or paperclip chains to represent the number *100*.

- Challenge students to read 100 books by the end of the year.

Hundred Chart

Directions: Write the numbers from 1 to 100 in the chart.

1									
			25						
									50
61									
									100

Hungry Alligators

Standard

Numbers and Operations—Understand numbers, ways of representing numbers, relationships among numbers, and number systems.

Objectives

Students will learn the mathematical symbols for *greater than, less than,* and *equal to* (>, <, =).

Students will practice using these symbols to compare and order whole numbers up to 100.

Materials

Hungry Alligators reproducible
Less Than, Greater Than reproducible
paper lunch bags
scissors, glue
crayons or markers
one hundred 4" x 6" index cards
construction paper squares (100 per student)

In this activity, students will compare numbers and associate a hungry alligator with the symbols for *greater than, less than,* and *equal to*. First, students will make alligator puppets and use them to play a number comparison game. Then they will create graphic organizers to demonstrate their knowledge of the concept.

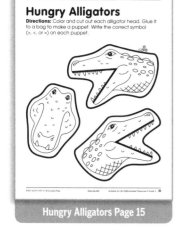

Hungry Alligators Page 15

◄ 1. To prepare for the activity, make a copy of the **Hungry Alligators reproducible (page 15)**. Color the patterns, cut them out, and glue each one to the bottom of a paper lunch bag to make alligator puppets. Write **>** on the puppet with its mouth open to the left, **<** on the puppet with its mouth open to the right, and **=** on the puppet with its mouth closed. Then number a set of 100 index cards from *1* to *100*. Make a few extra cards with the same number, such as two 50s and two 12s.

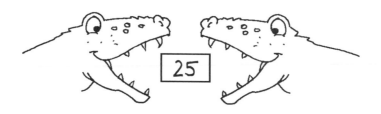

2. Show students the three puppets and tell them that the alligators are very hungry. Explain that the alligators will be given a choice of two things to eat and will always choose the larger of the two.

3. Choose two numbers from your stack of index cards, and display them on the chalkboard rail. Be sure to put the larger number on the left. Ask students which number is larger. Then place your *greater than* alligator between the two numbers. Point out the symbol written on the bag, and tell students that it means *greater than*. Read the entire number sentence aloud. For example: *25 is greater than 15.*

4. Point out how the alligator's open mouth resembles the *greater than* symbol and is pointing toward the larger number so he can eat it! Repeat the activity, this time placing the smaller number on the left. Place the *less than* alligator between the numbers, and read aloud the resulting number sentence. For example: *15 is less than 25.* Explain that the alligator's open mouth is still pointing toward the larger of the two numbers but is read as *less than* when pointed in this direction.

5. Let students take turns selecting numbers from the stack and choosing which alligator to put between them. Then introduce the concept of *equal to*. Place two index cards with the same number on the chalkboard rail and the *equal to* alligator between them. Have students demonstrate this concept as well.

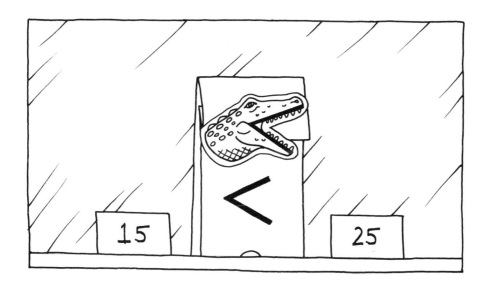

6. Give students a copy of the Hungry Alligators reproducible so they can make their own alligator puppets. Then give each student 100 squares of construction paper, and have them number the squares from 1 to 100.

7. Have students play the Hungry Alligator game with partners. Players shuffle their number squares, place them facedown in a stack, and turn over the top square. Players then take turns using their alligator puppets to compare the numbers. The player who flips over the larger number keeps both squares. If equal numbers are shown, the players flip over one more square and compare those two numbers. The player who flips the larger number collects all four squares. The game ends when all the squares are used. The player with the most squares wins.

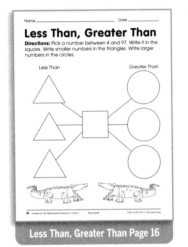

Less Than, Greater Than Page 16

8. Give students a copy of the **Less Than, Greater Than reproducible (page 16)**. In the center square, have each student write a number that is greater than 4 but less than 97. Then have students exchange papers and, in a triangle, write one number that is less than the number in the square. Have students continue trading papers with different classmates until each triangle has a number less than that in the square and each circle has a number greater than that in the square. Have students collect their original papers and check the accuracy of their classmates' work.

Ideas for More Differentiation

- Have beginning mastery students work in pairs to count and compare sets of real objects. Ask them to draw pictures to show their work.

- Have students with a high degree of mastery roll two dice to create two-digit numbers. For example, by rolling a 6 and a 2, the numbers 62 and 26 can be created. Ask students to write the numbers and use the appropriate symbols to compare them.

Extend the Activity

Have students look through grocery ads and find things that have equivalent costs. For example, grapes and tomatoes might both cost $1.99 per pound. Set a price, such as $5.00, and see how many things students can find that cost less than that amount and how many things they can find that cost more.

Hungry Alligators

Directions: Color and cut out each alligator head. Glue it to a bag to make a puppet. Write the correct symbol (>, <, or =) on each puppet.

Less Than, Greater Than

Directions: Pick a number between 4 and 97. Write it in the square. Write smaller numbers in the triangles. Write larger numbers in the circles.

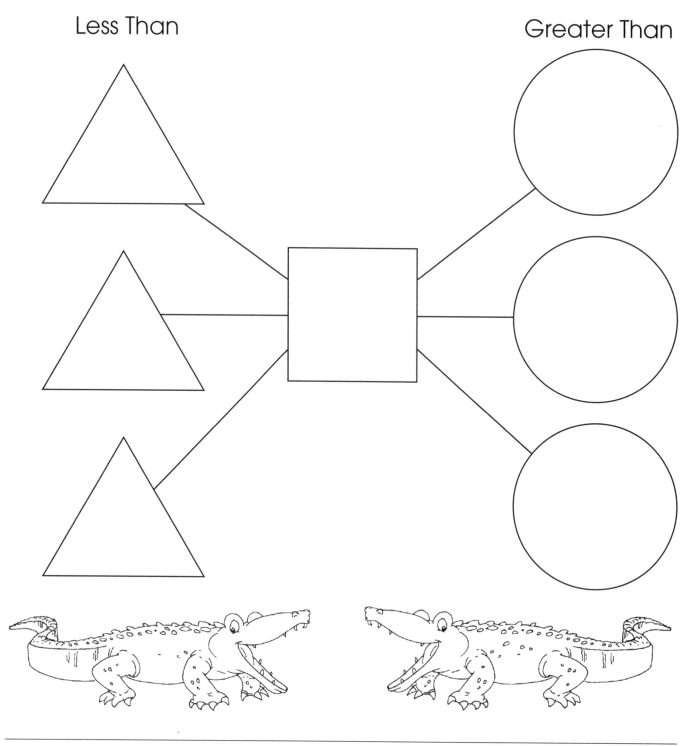

Less Than

Greater Than

Fact Wheels

Standard
Numbers and Operations—Understand meanings of operations and how they relate to one another.

Objective
Students will memorize math facts and see the inverse relationships between addition and subtraction problems.

Materials
Fact Families reproducible
66 empty toilet paper tubes
rulers, pencils, dark colored markers

Centers are a great way for students to practice learned skills. Centers allow students to work at their own pace and ability level. They also help students take responsibility for their own learning and increase their sense of independence.

1. Collect 66 empty toilet paper tubes, and distribute some of them to students. Give students a copy of the **Fact Families reproducible (page 19)**.

2. Demonstrate for students how to make a fact wheel. Invite them to make fact wheels as you work through the steps together. Be sure each student uses a different fact family for his or her wheel. On the Fact Families reproducible, cross out fact families as they are used.

   a. Use pencil to mark four sections around one end of the cardboard tube. This shows where you will write your equations.

   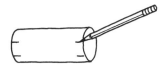

   b. At each mark, use a ruler to draw a pencil line from one end of the toilet paper tube to the other. This will make the rows where you will write the facts.

   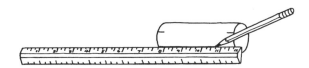

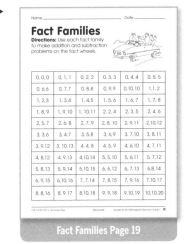

Fact Families Page 19

c. Use a marker to write the equations from one fact family on each line.

d. Cross off the numbers you used from the Fact Families page.

3. After the first batch of fact wheels are made, place the remaining cardboard tubes, rulers, pencils, and markers in the math center. Allow students to work individually or in pairs to make more fact wheels. Assist as needed. Make sure they cross off the numbers they use on the Fact Families page. This ensures that no fact family is duplicated and that all fact families have a fact wheel.

4. After all 66 wheels are made, have students visit the center to work with them. Students select a wheel and hold with their right thumb covering the answer as they read the problem. After giving answers, students can move their thumb to check the answers.

Ideas for More Differentiation

- Have high-degree mastery students work in pairs to quiz each other on fact families. Have one student say a number less than or equal to 20. Then his or her partner names three numbers to create a fact family for that number.

- Have beginning mastery students group the fact wheels to show how many different ways there are to arrive at a given sum. For example, there are seven different addition problems that result in a sum of 6.

Extend the Activity

Have students make mobiles that represent different fact families. Have them cut out shapes, such as triangle or circles, write the numbers for the fact families on the shapes, and then tie the shapes to coat hangers. Use fishing line to hang the mobiles around the classroom.

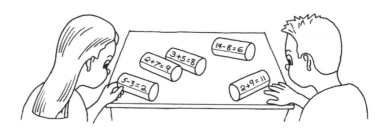

Fact Families

Directions: Use each fact family to make addition and subtraction problems on the fact wheels.

0, 0, 0	0, 1, 1	0, 2, 2	0, 3, 3	0, 4, 4	0, 5, 5
0, 6, 6	0, 7, 7	0, 8, 8	0, 9, 9	0, 10, 10	1, 1, 2
1, 2, 3	1, 3, 4	1, 4, 5	1, 5, 6	1, 6, 7	1, 7, 8
1, 8, 9	1, 9, 10	1, 10, 11	2, 2, 4	2, 3, 5	2, 4, 6
2, 5, 7	2, 6, 8	2, 7, 9	2, 8, 10	2, 9, 11	2, 10, 12
3, 3, 6	3, 4, 7	3, 5, 8	3, 6, 9	3, 7, 10	3, 8, 11
3, 9, 12	3, 10, 13	4, 4, 8	4, 5, 9	4, 6, 10	4, 7, 11
4, 8, 12	4, 9, 13	4, 10, 14	5, 5, 10	5, 6, 11	5, 7, 12
5, 8, 13	5, 9, 14	5, 10, 15	6, 6, 12	6, 7, 13	6, 8, 14
6, 9, 15	6, 10, 16	7, 7, 14	7, 8, 15	7, 9, 16	7, 10, 17
8, 8, 16	8, 9, 17	8, 10, 18	9, 9, 18	9, 10, 19	10, 10, 20

Math Theater

Standards

Algebra—Represent and analyze mathematical situations and structures using algebraic symbols.

Use mathematical models to represent and understand quantitative relationships.

Objectives

Students will identify key words in story problems to determine the operation needed to solve the problem.

Students will use addition and subtraction to solve story problems.

Materials

Math Theater reproducible

overhead projector

transparencies

This activity will appeal to students who represent many of Howard Gardner's multiple intelligences. Visual/linguistic learners will benefit from math problems being presented as stories. Logical/mathematical learners will shine as they work with numbers. Visual/spatial learners will appreciate the opportunity to draw out the solutions to problems. And bodily/kinesthetic and interpersonal learners will thrive by being in the spotlight during dramatic role-playing.

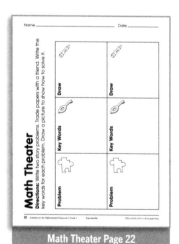

Math Theater Page 22

1. Make several overhead transparencies of the **Math Theater reproducible (page 22)**. Develop a set of simple addition and subtraction story problems, incorporating the names of your students. (Make sure every student is named at least once.) Write the problems on the transparencies.

2. Put one of the transparencies on the overhead projector. Pick a story problem from the transparency, and read it aloud. Have students who are named in the problem come to front of the classroom.

3. Have these students identify the key words in the story. Key words would include numbers used to solve the problem and any words that indicate whether the solution requires addition or subtraction. Ask the students to underline the key words and write them in the box next to the story problem.

4. Then invite the students to act out the story. Encourage them to use props to help illustrate the action.

5. Finally, have the students draw a picture to show how the problem was solved, write the equation for the problem, and, in the last box on the transparency, write a sentence that answers the story's question.

6. After solving each problem as a group, give each student a copy of the Math Theater reproducible. Have students write their own story problems and then exchange papers with a partner to solve.

Ideas for More Differentiation

- Allow beginning writers to use rebus-style pictures when writing story problems. Or, have them dictate to a teacher's aide.

- Let more advanced writers make posters for the class that show commonly used key words for addition and subtraction problems.

Extend the Activity

Have students work in groups to present short skits that dramatize mathematical story problems. Encourage them to use costumes and props for their skits.

Math Theater

Directions: Write two story problems. Trade papers with a friend. Write the key words for each problem. Draw a picture to show how to solve it.

Problem	Key Words	Draw
Problem	Key Words	Draw

Money Match

Standards

Numbers and Operations—Understand numbers, ways of representing numbers, relationships among numbers, and number systems. Compute fluently and make reasonable estimates.

Objectives

Students will add numbers to determine the value of sets of coins. Students will match different sets of coins that have equivalent values.

Materials

Money Match reproducibles
set of real or plastic coins for each group of four (4 quarters, 10 dimes, 20 nickels, 25 pennies)

First graders enjoy learning about the value of money. They understand that money is used to buy things, and knowing how to accurately count coins gives them a sense of accomplishment and power over their world. In this activity, students use real coins and pictures of coins to play a cooperative memory match game.

1. Duplicate a set of **Money Match reproducibles (pages 25–26)** for each team. Cut apart and laminate the cards.

2. Begin the activity by reviewing with students the value of a penny, nickel, dime, and quarter. Present a monetary value, such as 53 cents. Ask volunteers to use the coins to demonstrate different ways of showing that value. Continue practicing with other monetary values until each student has a change to participate.

3. Divide the class into teams of four. Give each team a set of Money Match cards and a set of coins (4 quarters, 10 dimes, 20 nickels, and 25 pennies).

4. Have teams shuffle their cards and place them facedown in rows. Each player chooses one card to flip over so four cards are showing. If two cards have matching values, all players take a turn using coins to show the matching value. The matching cards are removed, and the nonmatching cards are placed facedown again.

5. Play continues until all matching cards have been found. Everyone wins because everyone has practiced adding money!

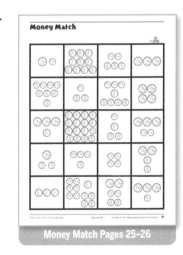

Money Match Pages 25–26

Ideas for More Differentiation

Set up a mock store in your classroom. Have beginning mastery students make price tags for the items in the store and design simple catalogs to advertise the items. Have high-degree mastery students use calculators to add up student purchases. Let them count the money they receive and make change from a cash drawer.

Extend the Activity

Let students look through toy catalogs and create wish lists of things they would like to purchase. Then have them use calculators to add up how much money they would need for everything on their lists.

Money Match

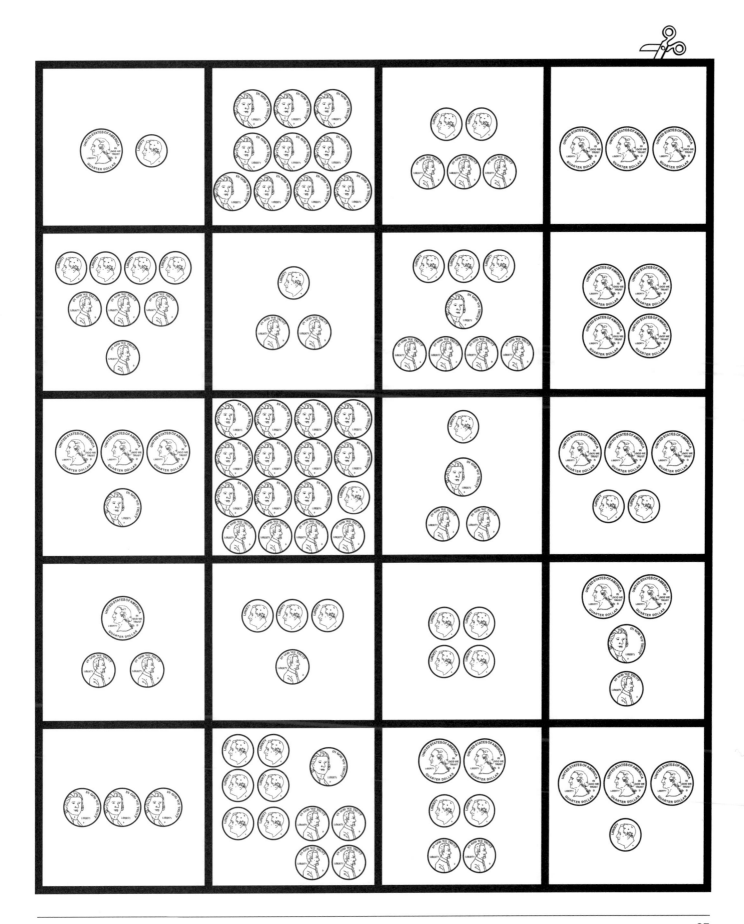

Money Match

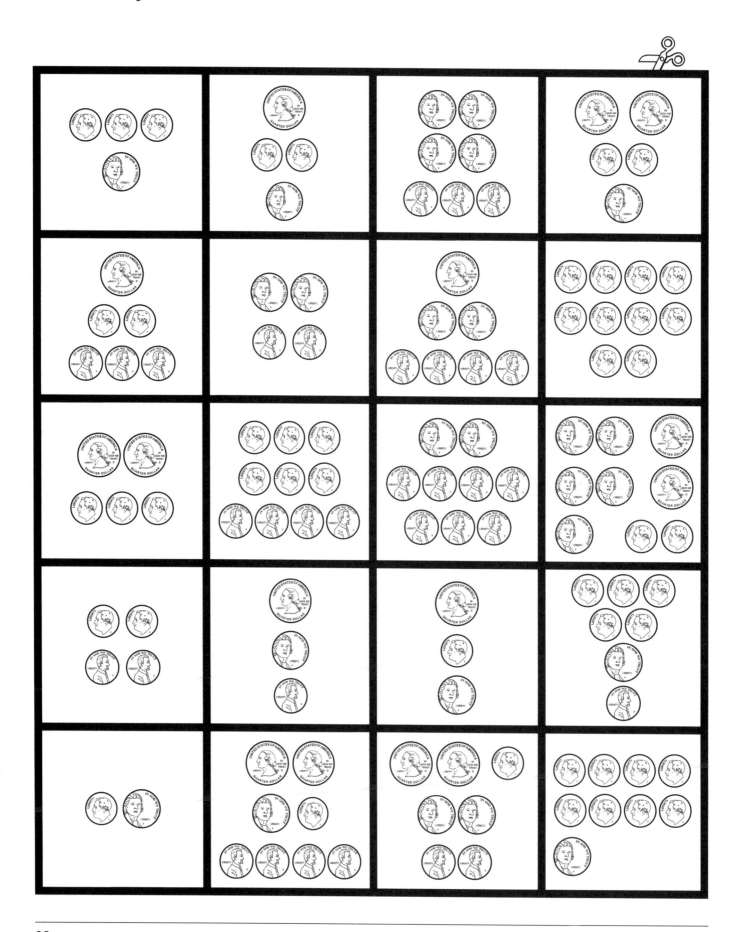

All Aboard the Geoboard Express

Standards

Geometry—Analyze characteristics and properties of two- and three-dimensional geometric shapes, and develop mathematical arguments about geometric relationships.

Communication—Use the language of mathematics to express mathematical ideas precisely.

Objective

Students will use geoboards to make geometric shapes and will record their experiences in a math journal.

Materials

The Geoboard Express reproducible
Geoboard Choice Board reproducible
construction paper
file box
5 x 5 geoboards
rubber bands in different colors and sizes

In this center activity, students practice working with geometric shapes. Using a choice board, they will select the learning activities they wish to complete. Then they will write about their work in their math journals.

1. Make five copies of **The Geoboard Express reproducible (page 29)** for each student. Staple the pages into a construction paper folder to

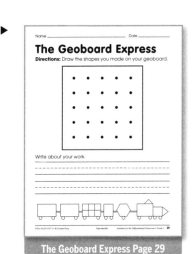

The Geoboard Express Page 29

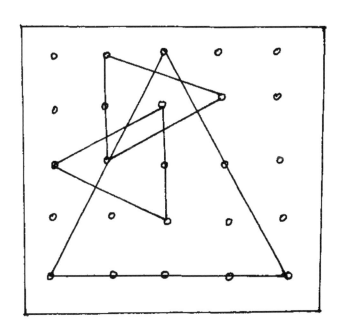

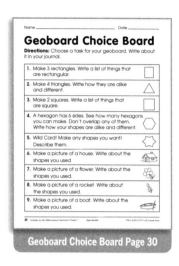
make a math journal. Make one copy of the **Geoboard Choice Board (page 30)** for each student. Staple the choice board to the front of each journal. Have students write their names on their journals and file them alphabetically in the math center.

2. Stock the math center with rubber bands (in different colors and sizes) and several square geoboards.

3. When students visit the center, invite each one to select one task from the choice board. They will use a geoboard and rubber bands to complete the task. Then they will write about it in their math journals and cross out the tasks on their choice boards.

4. Allow students to work in the center during specific times or when they have extra time between assignments and other projects. Be sure each student has adequate time to complete at least five tasks on the choice board.

Ideas for More Differentiation

Have students use pattern blocks to make pictures of different objects and then trace the block pictures onto construction paper. Ask high-degree mastery students to write the names of the shapes they used to make the pictures. Let beginning mastery students tell a partner about the shapes they used.

Extend the Activity

Invite students to go on a scavenger hunt for different geometric shapes. Give them a list of items to search for, such as a white circle or a red square. Let students work in teams to find the items. Award a small prize to the first team to complete the scavenger hunt.

The Geoboard Express

Directions: Draw the shapes you made on your geoboard.

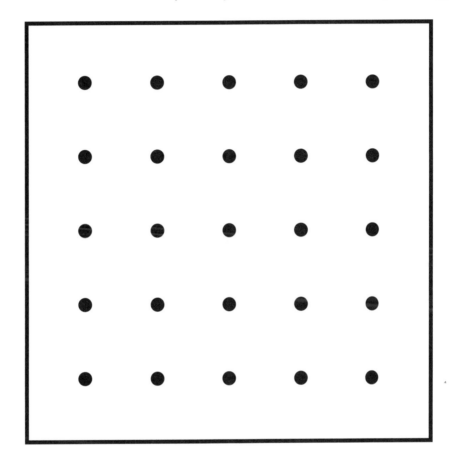

Write about your work.

_____

- -

_____

_____

- -

_____

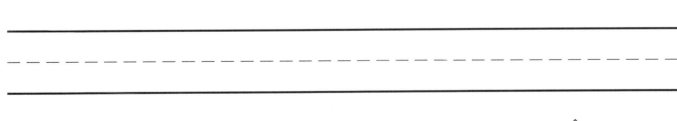

Name _____ Date _____

Geoboard Choice Board

Directions: Choose a task for your geoboard. Write about it in your journal.

---

1. Make 3 rectangles. Write a list of things that are rectangular.

---

2. Make 4 triangles. Write how they are alike and different.

---

3. Make 2 squares. Write a list of things that are square.

---

4. A hexagon has 6 sides. See how many hexagons you can make. Don't overlap any of them. Write how your shapes are alike and different.

---

5. Wild Card! Make any shapes you want! Describe them.

---

6. Make a picture of a house. Write about the shapes you used.

---

7. Make a picture of a flower. Write about the shapes you used.

---

8. Make a picture of a rocket. Write about the shapes you used.

---

9. Make a picture of a boat. Write about the shapes you used.

CHAPTER 2

Science

Investigation Station

Standard
Physical Science—Understand properties of objects and materials.

Objective
Students will learn that materials come in different forms (solids, liquids, and gases).

Materials
Learning Log reproducible
collection of solid objects in different shapes and sizes
water
plastic containers
measuring cups
several partially inflated balloons
balance scale
ruler
measuring tape
magnifying glass
microscope with slides
chart paper, construction paper

Strategies
Structured center

Inquiry

In this activity, students explore different forms of matter. Working in the learning center, they investigate a variety of materials in order to develop their own definitions of the terms *solid, liquid,* and *gas*. They are responsible for their own learning and will record their activities on a learning log.

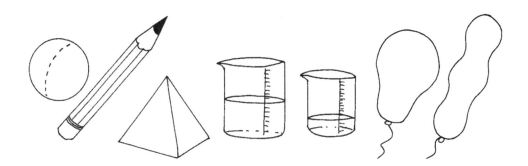

1. Display a variety of solid objects, different containers filled with liquid, and a few partially inflated balloons. Allow time for students to observe the items. Then ask: *What can you tell me about these objects?* Record their responses on chart paper.

2. Point to each set of objects and describe the sets as solids, liquids, or gases. (Explain that the balloons are filled with air, which is a gas.) Move the items to your Science Investigation Station, and tell students that they will conduct an investigation to answer the questions: *What is a solid? What is a liquid? What is a gas?*

3. Stock the center with objects from the materials list and a class set of **Learning Log reproducibles (page 33)**. Have students use the magnifying glass and microscope to study the objects. Encourage them to weigh and measure the materials and to manipulate them into different shapes. Have students record their tasks and observations in their Learning Log.

4. After all students have had a chance to work in the center, invite them to share observations. Record each student's contributions on chart paper, and compare it to the chart you created in Step 1.

5. Finally, work together to develop a definition for each state of matter. Record the definitions on sheets of construction paper, and hang them in the science center. Invite students to decorate the signs with pictures fitting the definitons.

Learning Log Page 33

Ideas for More Differentiation

Have more advanced students create charts to compare and contrast the three forms of matter. Have beginning mastery students draw pictures of different solids and liquids. (Avoid asking students to draw pictures of gases since they are invisible.)

Extend the Activity

Let students explore how the properties of matter change with heating or cooling. Have them place a bowl of ice cubes in a sunny place and observe how the warmth of the sun turns the solid ice into liquid water. When the water evaporates, explain to students that it didn't just disappear but turned into an invisible gas.

Name ______________________________ Date ____________

Learning Log

Directions: Work with solids, liquids, and gases. How do they feel? What do they look like? Draw pictures to show what you did. Write about it.

Solids	Liquids	Gases
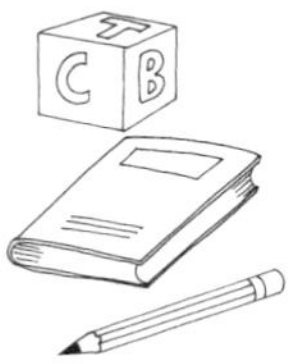	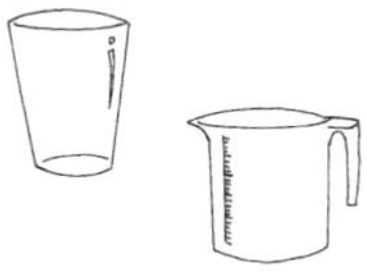	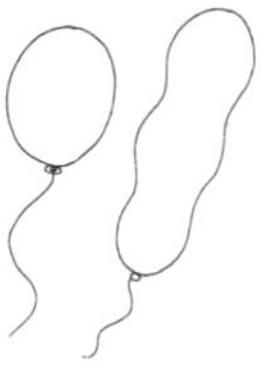

What is a solid? ______________________________

What is a liquid? ______________________________

What is a gas? ______________________________

A Habitat Is Home

Strategies

Cooperative group learning

Structured project

Choice board

Standard

Life Science—Understand organisms and environments.

Objective

Students will learn that plants and animals live in different kinds of environments and have a variety of features that help them survive.

Materials

Show What You Know reproducible

Habitat Planner reproducible

It's Your Choice reproducible

nature books and magazines featuring different animals and habitats

Most students love animals and are motivated to learn about them. In this activity, they form groups based on their common interests in particular animals. Students will gather information about the animal's habitat and how the animal is specially adapted to live in that habitat.

1. Display a collection of nature books and magazines that feature a variety of animals. Encourage students to look through the materials during free time.

2. Tell students they will select animals to research. Group them by the animals they choose. If groups are larger than four or five students, help them form smaller groups, and encourage any newly formed groups to choose different animals.

3. Help students come up with inventive group names based on their animals, such as *Terrific Tigers* or *Diving Dolphins*. Then have them make and decorate a folder to hold their work during the course of the project.

4. Give each group a copy of the **Show What You Know**, **Habitat Planner**, and **It's Your Choice reproducibles (pages 36–38)**. Ask groups to complete the first two sections of the KWL Chart on the Show What You Know reproducible. Work with each group individually if they need help. Then have them put the page in their group folder.

5. Explain that groups are responsible for learning the answers to the questions on the Project Planner and teaching the rest of the class about the animal they chose.

6. Provide blocks of class time for groups to research information for the Project Planner. Encourage students to use a variety of sources, including encyclopedias, books, magazines, and the Internet. Have them record the information and store it in their group folder.

7. After research is finished, call students' attention to the It's Your Choice page. Enlarge and post a copy on the board. Go over each choice with students, making sure they understand how to complete each one. Tell groups which projects they all must complete. Then allow them to choose another two or three projects, as well.

8. Invite each group to present its animal and habitat to the class. They can use projects completed from the Choice Board to teach the class about their chosen animal.

9. Have students finish the project by completing the last section of the KWL Chart and turning in their group folders.

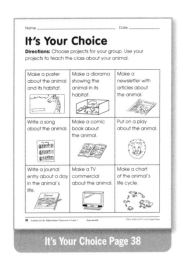

It's Your Choice Page 38

Ideas for More Differentiation

Assign roles for the cooperative groups that support each student's academic and social strengths. Students with a higher degree of mastery can be responsible for reading information to the group, whereas beginning mastery students can write schedules and draw pictures. Extroverted students can be the group's cheerleaders and keep everyone focused while introverted students manage the group's resources and time.

Extend the Activity

Have students make invitations to invite parents, friends, and school staff to view the presentations.

Name _____ Date _____

Show What You Know

Directions: Choose an animal. Write what you know about it. Write what you want to learn.

_____

Our animal is _____

What We KNOW About Our Animal	What We WANT TO KNOW About Our Animal	What We LEARNED About Our Animal

Habitat Planner

Directions: Learn about an animal. Then answer these questions.

1. What does the animal look like?

_____

- - - - - - - - - - - - - - - - - -

_____

_____

- - - - - - - - - - - - - - - - - -

_____

Draw a picture.

2. Where does it live?

_____

- -

_____

3. What does it eat?

_____

- -

_____

4. What other plants and animals live in its habitat?

_____

- -

_____

5. How does it protect itself?

_____

- -

_____

Name _____ Date _____

It's Your Choice

Directions: Choose projects for your group. Use your projects to teach the class about your animal.

Make a poster about the animal and its habitat. 	Make a diorama showing the animal in its habitat. 	Make a newsletter with articles about the animal. 
Write a song about the animal. 	Make a comic book about the animal. 	Put on a play about the animal. 
Write a journal entry about a day in the animal's life. 	Make a TV commercial about the animal. 	Make a chart of the animal's life cycle. 

What We Need

Standards
Life Science—Understand characteristics of organisms.
Understand organisms and environments.

Objective
Students will learn the basic needs of plants and animals.

Materials
What We Need Game Cards reproducibles
construction paper
glue
scissors

Strategies
Focus activity

Rehearsal

This simple, engaging activity focuses students' attention on what plants and animals need to survive by discussing the basic needs of people. Many students will mention things they want (e.g., *watching TV, playing sports, using a computer*) as well as things they need. Encourage them to distinguish between needs and wants and compare the needs of people with the needs of plants and animals. Students then pair off for a fun card game to help them retain their learning.

1. Begin by asking students: *What do you need in order to live?* List their responses on chart paper. Then talk about the difference between needs and wants. Have students evaluate their original list and determine which things are truly needs (*food, water, shelter, clothing*) and which are wants (*TV, computer, toys*).

2. Ask students to look at their needs and compare them to the needs of plants and animals. Point out that all plants and animals need food and water but not clothing. They have warm coats and other skin coverings to protect them. Most animals need some kind of shelter or home. Plants get light and food from the sun.

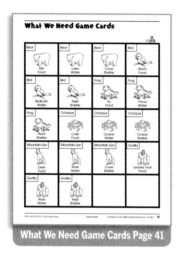

What We Need Game Cards Page 41

3. Reinforce learning by having student pairs play a card game about needs. Give each pair a copy of the **What We Need Game Cards reproducibles (pages 41–42)**. Help students glue the reproducibles onto sheets of construction paper and cut out the game cards.

4. In this game, there are three cards for each plant or animal shown. The object of the game is to collect sets of cards that show the same plant or animal with all three of its needs.

   a. To play, a student shuffles the cards and deals each player five cards. Place the remaining cards facedown in a pile. Turn over the top card, and place it next to the deck.

   b. Players take turns drawing one new card from the *draw* pile (facedown cards) or from the *discard* pile (faceup cards).

   c. After each draw, players must discard one card. If players have three cards that show the same plant or animal, they lay them down faceup.

   d. All cards in the discard pile should be visible. If players see a card they need in the discard pile, they must take all of the cards in front of that card and discard one.

   e. The game is over when one player has played or discarded all the cards in his or her hand. The player with the most sets of three wins.

Ideas for More Differentiation

Have high-degree mastery students make Venn diagrams to compare the foods they eat to the foods an animal eats. Beginning mastery students can collect animal pictures and classify them into groups based on what they eat (carnivores—meat-eaters, herbivores—plant-eaters, or omnivores—meat- and plant-eaters).

Extend the Activity

Ask students to plant different types of seeds. Have them give water to some and not to others. Have them place some of the seeds in sunlight and some in the dark. Let students observe and record what happens to the plants.

What We Need Game Cards

Bear	Bear	Bear	Bird
Fish Food	Lake Water	Cave Shelter	Worm Food

Bird	Bird	Frog	Frog
Birdbath Water	Nest Shelter	Fly Food	Pond Water

Frog	Octopus	Octopus	Octopus
Plant Shelter	Crab Food	Ocean Water	Ocean Shelter

Mountain Lion	Mountain Lion	Mountain Lion	Gorilla
Deer Food	River Water	Cave Shelter	Leaves, Fruit Food

Gorilla	Gorilla		
River Water	Nest Shelter		

What We Need Game Cards

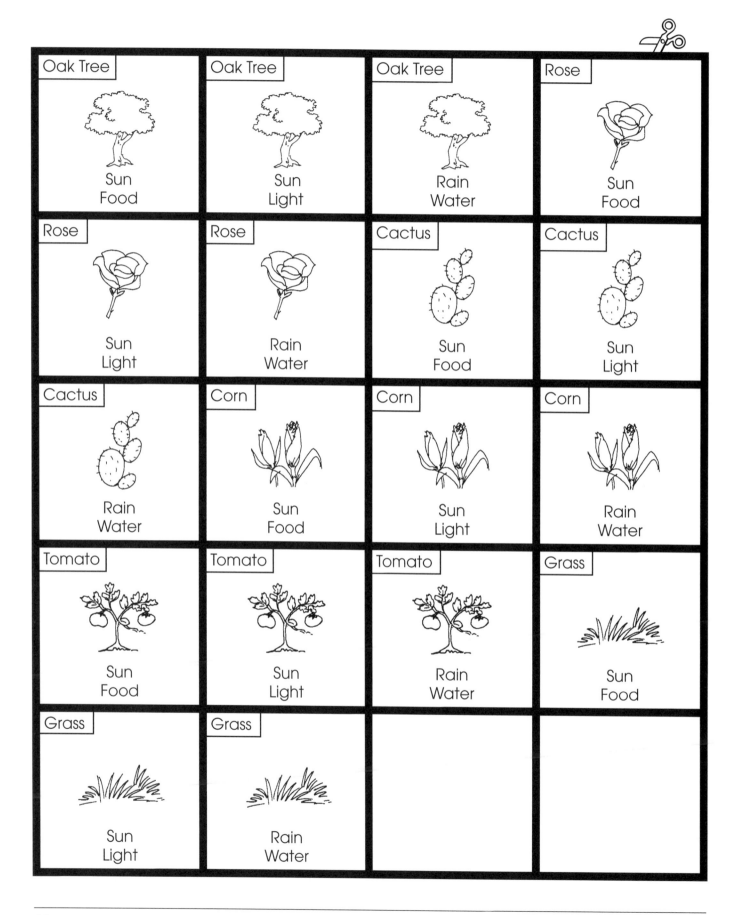

Oak Tree	Oak Tree	Oak Tree	Rose
Sun Food	Sun Light	Rain Water	Sun Food

Rose	Rose	Cactus	Cactus
Sun Light	Rain Water	Sun Food	Sun Light

Cactus	Corn	Corn	Corn
Rain Water	Sun Food	Sun Light	Rain Water

Tomato	Tomato	Tomato	Grass
Sun Food	Sun Light	Rain Water	Sun Food

Grass	Grass		
Sun Light	Rain Water		

Reproducible   978-1-4129-5337-5 • © Corwin Press

Weather and Seasons

Standard
Earth Science—Understand changes in the earth and sky.

Objective
Students will name the four seasons and describe how the weather changes with each season.

Materials
The Seasons of Arnold's Apple Tree by Gail Gibbons
photos of trees during different seasons
construction paper (light blue, brown, green, orange, red, yellow)
craft materials (fabric and felt scraps, yarn, buttons)
glue
scissors

In this activity, students observe photographs of trees in different seasons, listen to a story about a tree, and then write their own seasonal tree stories. Verbal/linguistic learners will benefit from the opportunity to listen, read, and write stories. Intrapersonal learners will appreciate working independently. Visual/spatial, naturalist, and bodily/kinesthetic students will all enjoy studying the photos and illustrations as well as constructing their own tree pictures.

1. Display photos of trees from different seasons. Ask students to compare the trees and name the seasons represented by each one.

2. Read aloud *The Seasons of Arnold's Apple Tree* by Gail Gibbons or another appropriate book.

3. Give each student three large sheets of light blue construction paper. Fold the papers in half, and staple them together to make a book. Invite students to design book covers, put their names in the

Strategies
Structured project

Multiple intelligences

title of the book, and write it on the front cover (e.g., *The Season's of Ana's Apple Tree*). If they like, students can also change the type of tree their book will be about. Then they can use paper scraps to make a picture of a tree on the front.

4. On the inside front cover, have students write a dedication. Then invite students to use construction paper scraps and other craft materials to make a picture of a tree on each right-hand page. Each tree should represent one season—spring, summer, fall, and winter.

5. Tell students to write a brief story for each tree on the left-hand pages of their books. Stories can be true or fictional but should reflect the season of each tree. They can write directly on the construction paper, or they can dictate stories to you while you type them on a computer. Glue the printed pages to the construction paper pages.

6. Encourage students to read their stories aloud in small groups. Store finished books in the classroom library for all to enjoy.

Ideas for More Differentiation

Let beginning mastery writers tape-record their stories. Attach a resealable plastic sandwich bag to the inside front cover of the book to hold the cassette tape. High-degree mastery students can collect leaves, study them under a microscope, and report their observations to the class.

Extend the Activity

Invite students to cut out pictures from clothing catalogs that show appropriate clothing for different types of weather. Have them work in seasonally named groups to create a group collage of seasonal clothing.

Weather in Our World

Standard
Earth Science—Understand changes in the earth and sky.

Objectives
Students will use simple weather instruments and record the daily temperature in their community.
Students will compare daily temperatures from cities around the world.

Materials
Weather in Our World reproducible
chart paper
outdoor thermometer

During this weather study, students compare the weather in their own community with that in other cities and create a graph to compare the average daily temperatures. They also explore how weather affects people's activities and create fact books to show what they learned.

1. Make a simple bar graph on chart paper to record the morning and afternoon temperatures. Write the dates for a one-month period along the bottom of the graph. (Leave enough room to record two temperatures for each date, morning and afternoon.) Write a range of temperatures common for your community along the left side of the graph. Title the graph *Our Local Weather*.

2. Show students how to read an outdoor thermometer, and each day, assign a different student to be the weather reporter. Have the reporter read the temperature in the morning and afternoon and report it to the class. Ask him or her to record the daily temperatures on the *Our Local Weather* graph.

3. Discuss with students the temperatures recorded on the class graph, and compare how changes in weather affect their daily activities. Ask students if they think other people around the world experience the same weather conditions.

4. Divide the class into small groups. Assign each group a city from a different region of the world. You may wish to use capital cities, such as Buenos Aires, Argentina; Ottawa, Canada; Canberra, Australia; Beijing, China; Cape Town, South Africa; and London, England. Or, use cities that represent the students' cultural makeup or personal interests. For a complete listing of the world's capitals, go to About: Geography at: *http://geography.about.com/od/countryinformation/a/capitals.htm.*

5. Have each group use an online weather reporting service, such as The Weather Channel (*www.weather.com*), to look up their city's daily weather for a ten-day period. Help groups make bar graphs to record the daily temperatures for their cities. Specify whether you want them to record the high temperature or the low temperature. If you wish, have them draw simple icons on their graphs to indicate sun, rain, snow, and clouds.

6. After ten days, compare and contrast the different graphs the groups created. Ask students: *Which city has the highest temperature for the time period? Which has the lowest? In which parts of the world is it raining or snowing?*

7. Allow groups to continue their investigations. They can use the Internet, library books, and encyclopedias to learn more about the people and activities in the areas they are studying. Give each group a copy of the **Weather in Our World reproducible (page 47)** to guide their research.

8. Finally, have groups use what they've learned to create a display about the city or country they studied. Help students write sentences about their area of the world and its weather. They should include a map of the country, a graph to show the weather, and pictures of the clothes people wear and the things they do. Invite groups to share their displays with the class.

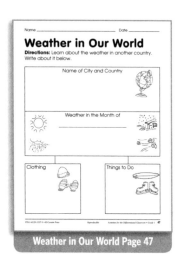

Weather in Our World Page 47

Name _____ Date _____

Weather in Our World

Directions: Learn about the weather in another country. Write about it below.

Name of City and Country

Weather in the Month of

Clothing

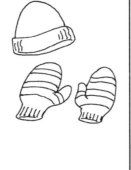

Things to Do

Social Studies

Gold Star Behavior

Standards

Understand the interactions among people, places, and environments. Understand individual development and identity.

Objectives

Students will learn to empathize with how others might feel in different situations.

Students will explain the importance of following the Golden Rule and demonstrate the use of good manners.

Materials

Gold Star Behavior reproducibles

yellow construction and butcher paper

gold stars, sequins, beads, glitter glue

decorative ribbon

small candies in gold wrapping

gift box and wrapping paper

chart paper

art supplies

It is often difficult for young children to put themselves in another person's place and to try to understand how he or she might feel. In this activity, students have the opportunity to practice this skill while role-playing various scenes. They will use different scenarios to demonstrate the difference between good manners and bad manners.

1. Ahead of time, write the Golden Rule on a sheet of yellow butcher paper: *Treat others as you would like to be treated*. Decorate the sheet with gold stars, sequins, beads, and glitter glue. Roll up the paper and tie it with a decorative ribbon. Place it in a gift box with small candies in gold wrapping, and gift-wrap it. Display the box so the whole class can see it.

2. Tell students there is a gift in the box that you will share with them and that they can share with everyone they meet. Tell them it is a gift they will keep for the rest of their lives. Ask a few students

to guess what it is. Then explain that they will open the box after they complete a few activities.

3. Ask students to explain the difference between good manners and bad manners and give a few examples. Write their responses on chart paper. For example: *It's good manners to wait your turn to speak, but it's bad manners to interrupt someone who's speaking.* Next, ask students to tell how they feel when people use bad manners. Use specific examples, such as *playing a game with someone who cheats,* or *eating with someone who talks with food in his or her mouth.*

4. Divide the class into small groups. Make a copy of the **Gold Star Behavior reproducibles (pages 50–51)**. Cut apart the scenario cards, and give one to each group. Have groups develop role plays for the scenarios on their cards. They should role-play the scenario showing bad manners and then a role-play the scenario showing good manners.

Gold Star Behavior Page 50

5. After all the role plays have been presented, lead a discussion about how the characters must have felt in the different scenarios. Ask students what this tells them about how they should treat others.

6. Choose a student to open the gift box and display the banner. Tell students that this saying is known as the *Golden Rule.* Following the Golden Rule shows respect for others and is a gift they can give to everyone. Give students a piece of candy from the gift box as a reward for using good manners and following the Golden Rule.

7. Provide yellow construction paper and various art supplies for students to use to make their own Golden Rule banners.

Ideas for More Differentiation

Let high-degree mastery writers make picture books about following the Golden Rule. Have them write about and draw pictures of different scenarios in which the rule is being followed.

Gold Star Behavior

Taking Turns

Playing Fair

Being a Good Sport

Gold Star Behavior

Being Kind

Being Polite

Being Helpful

 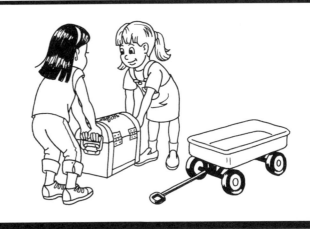

Where in the World?

Strategies
Focus activity

Rehearsal

Standard
Understand the interactions among people, places, and environments.

Objective
Students will use cardinal directions to describe the location of oceans and continents on a map or globe.

Materials
Where in the World? reproducible
world wall map
inflatable globe
chart paper

Break up the routine in your classroom with this engaging focus activity! Grab students' attention by allowing them to toss an inflatable globe around the room. The physical nature of the activity will help them focus on learning the names and locations of the continents and oceans.

1. Display a world wall map. Ask students to point out features with which they are familiar. Indicate the directions *north*, *south*, *east*, and *west*. Use those directions to describe the locations of the continents and the oceans. For example: *The Pacific Ocean is west of North America.*

2. Give students a copy of the **Where in the World? reproducible (page 54)**. Tell them that they will listen to clues about the location of a continent or ocean and then use the map to find the place being described.

3. Start the game by tossing an inflatable globe into the air and catching it. Look at where your right thumb is on the globe. Then rotate the globe so the North Pole is at the top. Based on the location of your thumb, tell students whether you have landed on an ocean or a continent. Then use cardinal directions to give clues about where you are. For example: *I am on a continent. My continent is east of North America and north of Africa.*

4. Encourage students to study their own maps to discover that you are describing Europe. Ask a volunteer to show where Europe is located on the wall map.

5. Next, toss the globe to a student. Invite him or her to repeat the process you demonstrated in Step 3. Have the student describe the location of the continent or ocean and choose a volunteer to identify the place on the wall map. Then have the student toss the globe to someone else. Continue playing until everyone has had a turn catching the globe and identifying a place on the wall map.

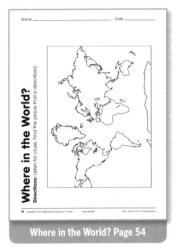

Where in the World? Page 54

Ideas for More Differentiation

Have beginning mastery students name the ocean or continent on which their right thumb landed, and let them call on volunteers to describe its location. Have high-degree mastery students use the wall map to identify specific countries within the continents.

Extend the Activity

Invite students to draw pictures of landmarks on a map of your community. Let them provide clues that describe the location of each landmark. For example: *This landmark is north of our school, east of the river, and south of Main Street.*

Name _____ Date _____

Where in the World?

Directions: Listen for clues. Find the place that is described.

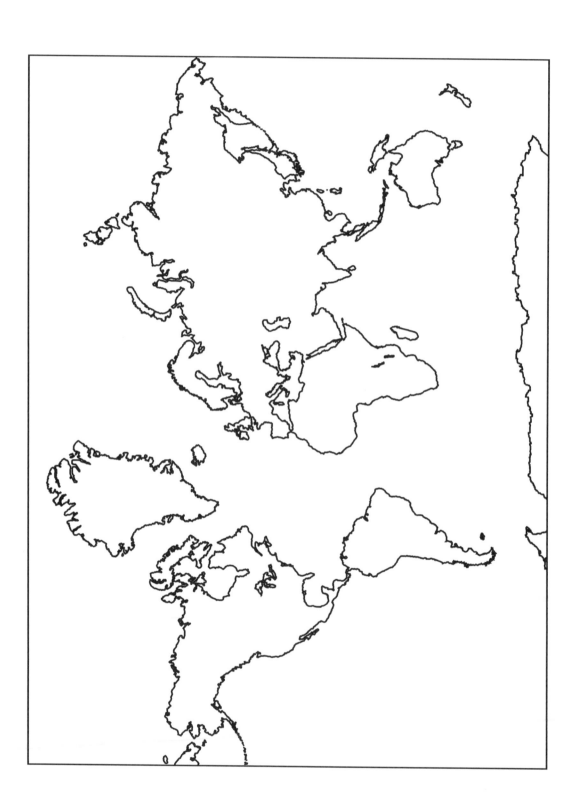

A Holiday Fair

Standard
Understand culture and cultural diversity.

Objective
Students will explain the meaning and customs behind traditional
United States and world holidays.

Materials
Make a Holiday Display reproducible
Holiday Choice Board reproducible
books about holidays
36" x 48" project display boards
art supplies

Strategies
Cooperative group learning

Choice board

Everyone loves a holiday, especially kids! In this activity, students not
only learn about holidays, but also plan their own special celebration.
Working in pairs or small groups, students choose activities to teach
others about the holidays they are studying. The project culminates with a
holiday fair packed with food, music, crafts, and fun!

1. Display your collection of books about various federal holidays.
   Select one or two books to read aloud each day.

2. Discuss with students what makes each holiday special and
   unique. Ask: *Why do we celebrate this holiday? What traditions
   do people follow for this holiday? Does your family do anything
   special for this holiday?*

3. Have students work in small groups, and assign each group one
   holiday. To make sure groups work together effectively, try to
   group students according to different abilities. For example, try to
   create groups that include a good reader, writer, artist,
   and manager.

Make a Holiday Display Page 57

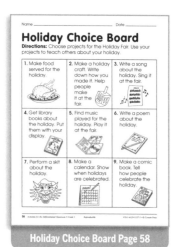

Holiday Choice Board Page 58

4. Tell groups they will design a holiday-fair booth. They will create a holiday display, following the directions on the **Make a Holiday Display reproducible (page 57)**. Then they will select other projects for their booths from the **Holiday Choice Board reproducible (page 58)**.

5. Go over the reproducibles with students, giving step-by-step instructions and answering questions. Give them plenty of class time to prepare for the fair. Assist each group with their project, and allow them access to library books and the Internet to learn about the holidays.

6. Invite parents, other classes, and staff members to attend the Holiday Fair. Cover tables with festive tablecloths, and have groups display their projects on the tables. Encourage guests to ask questions and share holiday stories and experiences.

Ideas for More Differentiation

Have students prepare a survey for their guests to complete. The survey can ask about favorite holidays and holiday traditions that people practice. After the fair, have students analyze and graph the results.

Extend the Activity

Encourage students to continue this study by having a multicultural fair. Invite students and parents to bring in different cultural foods from home to share with the class. They can share special family holiday stories and traditions. Celebrations might include Chinese New Year, Ramadan, Boxing Day, Hanukkah, and Children's Day.

Make a Holiday Display

Step 1: Use stencils to write the name of your holiday on construction paper. Cut out the letters. Glue them at the top of your display board.

Step 2: Use stencils to write the date the holiday is celebrated on construction paper. Cut out the letters and numbers. Glue them under the name of your holiday.

Step 3: Write sentences about why the holiday is celebrated. Glue the paper under the date.

Step 4: Think about things that happen during the holiday.

- Are special foods eaten?
- Are there parades or parties?
- Are decorations used?
- Do people make or give gifts?

Write or draw pictures about these things. Glue your papers to the side panels of your display board.

Holiday Choice Board

Directions: Choose projects for the Holiday Fair. Use your projects to teach others about your holiday.

1. Make food served for the holiday. 	**2.** Make a holiday craft. Write down how you made it. Help people make it at the fair. 	**3.** Write a song about the holiday. Sing it at the fair. 
4. Get library books about the holiday. Put them with your display. 	**5.** Find music played for the holiday. Play it at the fair. 	**6.** Write a poem about the holiday. 
7. Perform a skit about the holiday. 	**8.** Make a calendar. Show when holidays are celebrated. 	**9.** Make a comic book. Tell how people celebrate the holiday.

From Field to Market

Standard

Understand how people organize for the production, distribution, and consumption of goods and services.

Strategies
Graphic organizer

Multiple intelligences

Objective

Students will use a graphic organizer and make a visual representation to demonstrate how goods are made and brought to market.

Materials

From Field to Market reproducible
books about the production and distribution of goods (see Book List)
chart paper
paper plates, brass fasteners
crayons or markers, rulers, scissors

Book List

There are many wonderful children's books that describe the process of bringing goods to market. Here are a few suggestions:
Extra Cheese, Please! Mozzarella's Journey from Cow to Pizza
by Cris Peterson
From Plant to Blue Jeans: A Photo Essay
by Arthur John L'Hommedieu
From Wheat to Pasta by Robert Egan
If It Weren't for Farmers by Allan Fowler
The Tortilla Factory by Gary Paulsen

Help students understand interconnectedness between themselves and the wider world. In this activity, students create a sequence wheel to demonstrate how products they use in everyday life come to be. Throughout the process, they learn about the specialized work people do to produce and distribute goods.

1. Start a KWL chart with students about the manufacturing and distribution of goods. Ask them what they know about how products such as milk or blue jeans are made. Record their responses under the *K* for *Know*. Ask them what they want to learn about the process, and record those responses under the *W* for *Want*. At the end of this unit, complete the last section of the chart by writing what was *Learned* under the *L*.

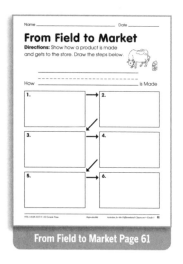

From Field to Market Page 61

2. Read aloud one or more books about the process of manufacturing and distributing goods. Then give students a copy of the **From Field to Market reproducible (page 61)**. Have them write or draw pictures to show the steps involved in getting a product made, transported, stored, and purchased.

3. Next, give each student two paper plates, a ruler, a brass paper fastener, scissors, and crayons or markers. Have students use the ruler and a marker or crayon to divide a paper plate into six equal sections. Then have them draw a picture in each section to illustrate the steps they showed on their graphic organizer. Remind students to rotate their plate so the pictures will appear right side up when the project is completed.

4. To finish the project, have students cut out a section from the second plate equal to one section on the first plate. Have them write a title on the top of the second plate and decorate it with pictures about the topic. Then fasten the two plates together in the center with the brass fastener. Students can rotate the top plate to reveal one step of the process at a time.

Ideas for More Differentiation

Have students study different types of jobs that are part of the creation of a product. Let high-degree mastery students write paragraphs about the jobs while beginning mastery students make a deck of trading cards illustrating the jobs.

Extend the Activity

Have students set up a production process to create a product they can sell. They might bake cookies or design bookmarks or greeting cards. Let students decide who will be responsible for manufacturing, distributing, and selling the products. Suggest that the money earned be donated to a local charity.

Name _____ Date _____

From Field to Market

Directions: Show how a product is made and gets to the store. Draw the steps below.

How _____ is Made

| 1. | → | 2. |

| 3. | → | 4. |

| 5. | → | 6. |

When I Was Young

Strategies

Authentic task

Graphic organizer

Standards

Understand culture and cultural diversity.

Understand the ways human beings view themselves in and over time.

Objective

Students will interview older family members and use a graphic organizer to examine how life has changed over time.

Materials

Interview Sheet reproducible

Then and Now Venn Diagram reproducible

artifacts from other generations (toys, clothes, books, photographs)

In this activity, students draw upon the rich experiences of older members of the community. They will learn about what life was like when their grandparents were children, and they will compare those experiences to their own. Many children may be surprised to learn that their grandparents didn't have home computers, microwave ovens, or DVD players when they were young. In fact, some of the grandparents may actually remember living in homes without televisions!

1. Help focus students' attention by displaying a few artifacts from their grandparents' generation, such as vinyl records, cardboard paper dolls, and saddle shoes. If possible, add to your display by borrowing old school textbooks or magazines and department

store catalogs from your local library or district office. Find and display photographs that show clothes, appliances, furniture, homes, and cars from that era.

2. Allow students to explore your display, and encourage them to discuss how they think some of the items were used and how they are alike and different from similar items used today.

3. Tell students that they will interview someone from their family or neighborhood who was a child 30 to 50 years ago.

4. Give students a copy of the **Interview Sheet reproducible (page 64)**. Read the categories shown on the sheet, and help students come up with sample interview questions for each topic. Then let students work independently to write one or two questions of their own. Circulate around the room, and assist as needed.

5. Allow students a week or two to complete their interviews. In the meantime, read and discuss picture books set in the 1940s, 1950s, 1960s, and 1970s. Invite students to compare life today with life during those times.

6. Give students a copy of the **Then and Now Venn Diagram (page 65)**. Demonstrate how to complete a Venn diagram on the board. Then have students complete the diagram, using information from their Interview Sheet to compare their life with that of the interviewee.

Interview Sheet Page 64

Ideas for More Differentiation

Allow beginning mastery students to work in small groups to generate a list of interview questions. Have high-degree mastery students interview each other and answer their questions as they apply to life today.

Extend the Activity

Invite a panel of older people (parents, grandparents) to come to your class to discuss what their childhoods were like. If possible, include a person who was born in each decade from the 1940s to 1980s. Invite students to ask questions and practice good listening skills.

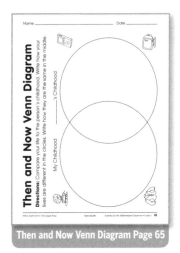

Then and Now Venn Diagram Page 65

Name _____ Date _____

Interview Sheet

Directions: Interview an older person about his or her childhood. Write one or two questions for each topic. Write the answers on another sheet of paper.

Person's Name: _____

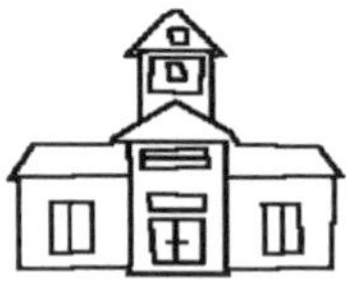

School
_____

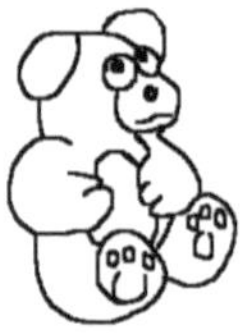

Toys
_____

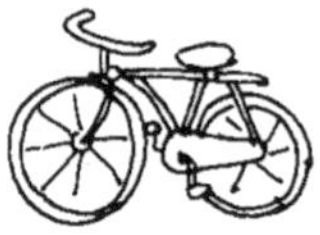

Recreation
_____

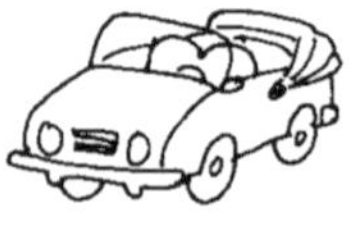

Transportation
_____

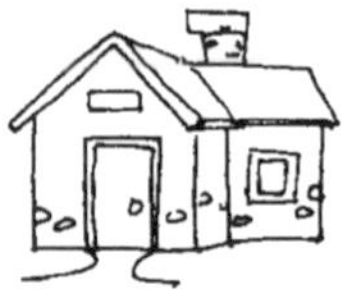

Family/Home
_____

Then and Now Venn Diagram

Directions: Compare your life to the person's childhood. Write how your lives are different in the circles. Write how they are the same in the middle.

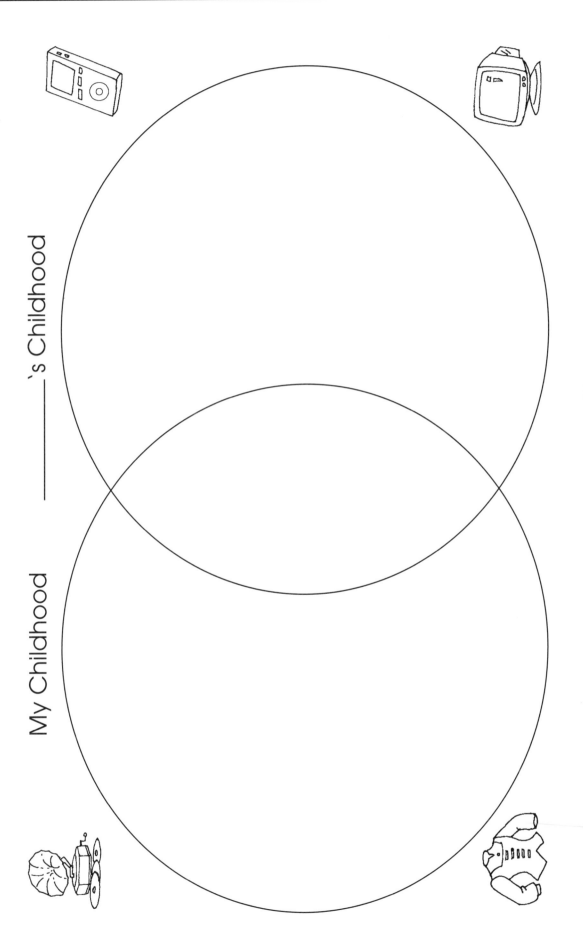

_____'s Childhood

My Childhood

CHAPTER 4

Language Arts

A Walk to the Park

Strategies
Sponge activity

Rehearsal

Standard
Apply a wide range of strategies to comprehend, interpret, evaluate, and appreciate texts. Draw on prior experience, interactions with other readers and writers, knowledge of word meaning and of other texts, word identification strategies, and understanding of textual features (e.g., sound-letter correspondence, sentence structure, context, graphics).

Objective
Students will demonstrate phonemic awareness by changing one letter in a given word to make a new word.

Materials
A Walk to the Park Game Board reproducibles
Playing the Game reproducible
file folders
glue
dice, game markers (pennies, paper clips, counters)

Turn learning into play with this fun phonics game. In this activity, students practice and hone their phonics skills. Through the use of an interactive board game, they read one-syllable words and identify letters that can be changed to make new words.

1. Assemble a game board for each pair of students. Copy the **A Walk to the Park Game Board reproducibles (pages 68–69)**, and glue

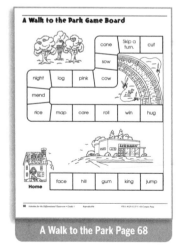

A Walk to the Park Page 68

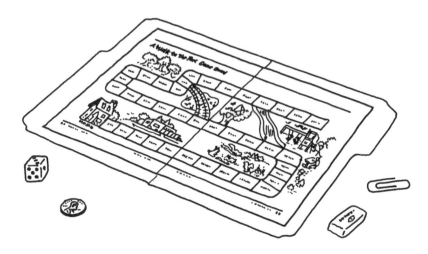

them to the inside of a file folder. Copy the **Playing the Game reproducible (page 70)**, and glue one set of instructions to the front of the file folder. Invite students and/or parent volunteers to color the game boards.

Playing the Game Page 70

2. To use this game as a simple sponge activity, call out a word and ask a student to change one letter in the word to make a new word. For example, *cow* can become *how*, and *how* can become *hot*. Challenge students to see how many new words they can make from the original word. Continue practicing as a group until you feel students are proficient enough to play A Walk to the Park on their own.

3. Review the rules of the game with students. Then invite student pairs to play the game independently.

Ideas for More Differentiation

Have beginning mastery students focus on changing only the initial letter in each word. High-degree mastery students can try to change a medial or ending letter (although not all the words on the game board can be changed in this way).

Extend the Activity

Have students make word chains to show that by changing one letter at a time, they can create many different words. Provide strips of construction paper. Have students choose a word to write on the first strip and then glue the ends of the strip together to make a loop. For each new word that is made, students can add a loop to the word chain.

A Walk to the Park Game Board

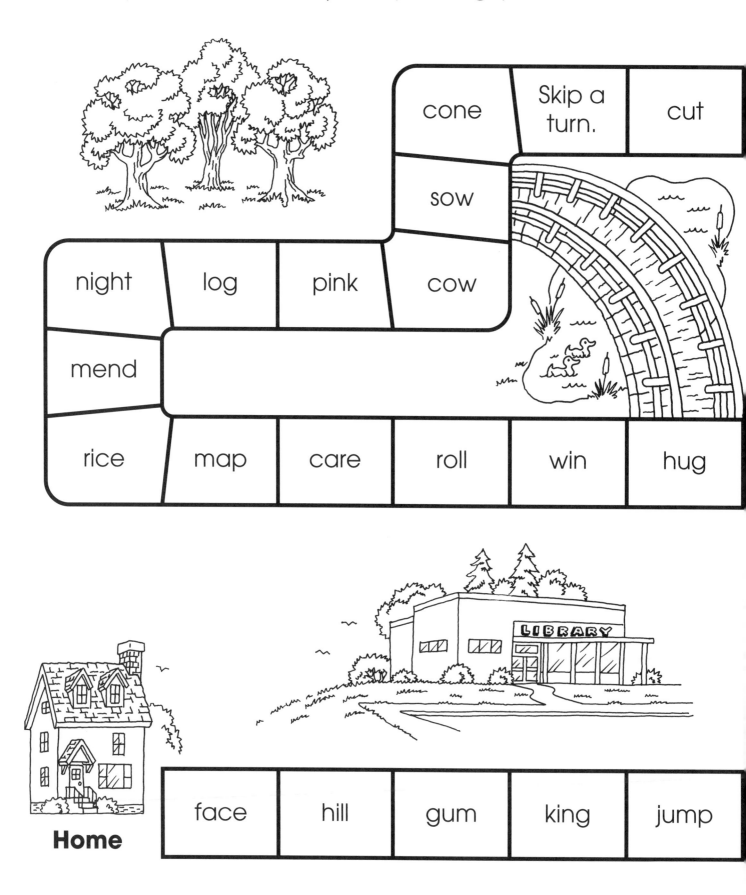

cone

Skip a turn.

cut

sow

night | log | pink | cow

mend

cow

rice | map | care | roll | win | hug

LIBRARY

Home

face | hill | gum | king | jump

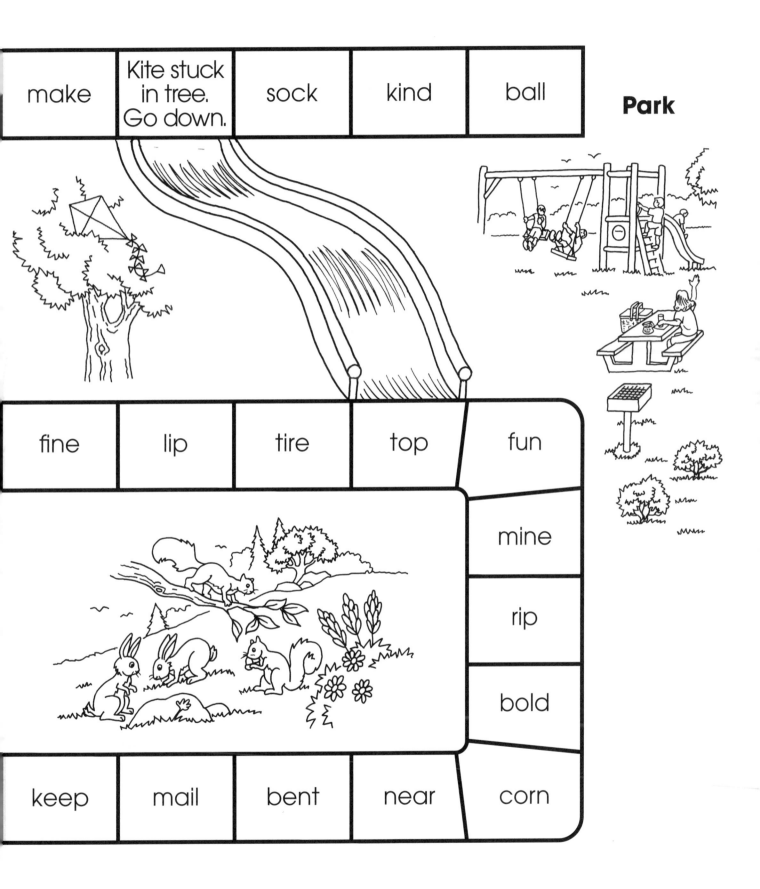

make | Kite stuck in tree. Go down. | sock | kind | ball

Park

fine | lip | tire | top | fun

mine

rip

bold

keep | mail | bent | near | corn

Playing the Game

How to Play:

1. Each player rolls the die. The player with the highest number goes first.

2. Roll the die. Move your marker that number of spaces forward.

3. Read aloud the word on the space where you land. Change one letter in the word to make a new word. If you cannot make a new word, go back to the last space you were on.

4. The next player takes a turn.

5. There are two special squares on the path:
   - If you land on a square that says, "Kite stuck in tree. Go down," follow the slide to the square below.
   - If you land on a square that says, "Skip a turn," skip one turn.

6. The player who gets to the park first wins the game!

Super Sunflowers

Standards

Apply a wide range of strategies to comprehend, interpret, evaluate, and appreciate texts. Draw on prior experience, interactions with other readers and writers, knowledge of word meaning and of other texts, word identification strategies, and understanding of textual features (e.g., sound-letter correspondence, sentence structure, context, graphics).

Apply knowledge of language structure, language conventions (e.g., spelling and punctuation), media techniques, figurative language, and genre to create, critique, and discuss print and nonprint texts.

Objective

Students will be able to identify and write compound words.

Materials

Super Sunflowers reproducible
construction paper (yellow, green, light brown)
butcher paper (blue, tan)
magazines, newspapers, dictionaries, books
tag board
scissors
glue
chart paper

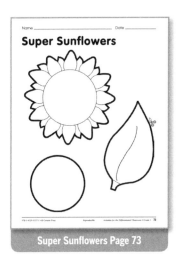

Super Sunflowers Page 73

Students will love working in this center and creating their own bulletin board display. Using paper sunflowers, they will create a garden to show off their knowledge of compound words.

1. Cover the top third of a bulletin board with blue butcher paper to make a sky. Cover the bottom two-thirds with tan butcher paper to make the ground.

2. Copy the **Super Sunflowers reproducible (page 73)**. Cut out the shapes and trace them onto tag board to make sunflower patterns. Make at least three sets of patterns.

3. Place the sunflower patterns, construction paper, scissors, and glue in a center near the bulletin board.

4. Discuss compound words with the class. Provide a few examples such as *sunflower, popcorn,* and *daydream.* Write examples on the board, and show how each word is made of two words that, when combined, make a new word with a different meaning.

5. Ask students to brainstorm a list of compound words. Let them look through dictionaries, magazines, newspapers, and books to find more compound words. Write students' suggestions on a sheet of chart paper. Post the list in the center.

6. Tell students that they will make a sunflower garden to show the compound words they know. Show them how to trace the flower patterns onto construction paper to make the flowers. Each flower should have a stem, two leaves, petals, and a center circle.

7. For each sunflower, tell students to do the following:

   • Write a complete compound word on the stem.

   • Write the first part of the compound word on one leaf.

   • Write the other part of the compound word on the other leaf.

   • In the center circle, draw a picture to illustrate the compound word.

8. As sunflowers are assembled, help students tape or staple them onto the bulletin board. Allow students to work independently in the center as they finish other class work.

Ideas for More Differentiation

Encourage beginning readers to practice reading the compound words on the sunflowers. Have them use their knowledge of phonics to decode each individual word, blend them, and read the compound. Invite more advanced readers to alphabetize the words and make a picture dictionary.

Extend the Activity

Have students draw pictures of butterflies, dragonflies, grasshoppers, and bumblebees to add to the bulletin board. If you wish, students can write more compound words on their drawings.

Super Sunflowers

Word Power

Standard

Apply a wide range of strategies to comprehend, interpret, evaluate, and appreciate texts. Draw on prior experience, interactions with other readers and writers, knowledge of word meaning and of other texts, word identification strategies, and understanding of textual features (e.g., sound-letter correspondence, sentence structure, context, graphics).

Objective

Students will name words that belong together in basic categories.

When you need students to line up for a new activity, whether it is going to the cafeteria for lunch or heading to the library, play this simple word game. As students name words that fit into specific categories, they are allowed to join the line.

1. Name a category, such as *clothes* or *food*. Tell students that you will start the game by saying a word that fits the category. Choose a word such as *sock*. Instruct students to listen to the word and identify the last sound they hear, /k/. The next person must choose a word that begins with the ending sound, /k/, such as *cap*. The next word would begin with the /p/ sound, such as *poncho*.

2. As each student offers a new word, he or she is allowed to get in line. If a student cannot name a new word, start a new category.

3. Continue playing until all students have contributed a word and lined up to move to the next activity.

Ideas for More Differentiation

Remove the phonics component for beginning mastery learners. Instead of having them choose words that begin with particular sounds, let them focus on the word category only. For high-degree mastery learners, choose categories with a narrower focus, such as *forest animals* rather than *animals*.

Extend the Activity

Invite students to play this game in small groups. Assign one person in each group to be the recorder. Have the recorder write down all the words used. When all groups are finished playing, award one point for each word that was not used by any other group. The group with the most points wins!

Story Sleuths

Standards

Read a wide range of print and nonprint texts to build an understanding of texts, of self, and of the cultures of the United States and the world; to acquire new information; to respond to the needs and demands of society and the workplace; and for personal fulfillment (includes fiction and nonfiction, classic, and contemporary works).

Apply a wide range of strategies to comprehend, interpret, evaluate, and appreciate texts. Draw on prior experience, interactions with other readers and writers, knowledge of word meaning and of other texts, word identification strategies, and understanding of textual features (e.g., sound-letter correspondence, sentence structure, context, graphics).

Strategies
Jigsaw

Cooperative group learning

Objective
Students will work in groups to identify and discuss story elements.

Materials
Story Sleuths reproducible
multiple copies of the same picture book
chart paper
construction paper, scissors, pencils, crayons, markers

In this cooperative group activity, every student gets to be an expert! After reading a picture book together, each student is assigned one story element. Student "detectives" then search for clues about their story element. Each detective shares what he or she learned so the group can retell the story.

1. Read a book aloud to students. Then talk about story elements: characters, setting, problem, and resolution. Ask students to look for details that tell about the story elements. Write their responses on chart paper. For each topic, ask the following questions:

   Characters: Who is the main character? Who are the other characters? What do the characters look and sound like? How do they behave? What do they like and dislike?

   Setting: Where does the story take place? In what time period is it set? What do the land and the buildings look like? How does the weather affect the story?

Problem: What problems happen in the story? Who faces the problems? How do the problems affect the characters? Does one problem turn into other problems?

Resolution: What steps do the characters take to solve the problems? How do the characters feel before and after solving the problems?

2. Read aloud another picture book to students. Make sure you have multiple copies of this book available.

3. Divide the class into groups of four. Give each group a copy of the **Story Sleuths reproducible (page 77)**. Have them cut the page into fourths. Assign each student one story element, and give him or her that section of the page. Have students glue this section to the top of a sheet of construction paper.

4. Have students regroup based on their assigned story elements. Give each new group at least one copy of the book. They will work together to look for clues about their story element. For example, the *character* group will look for details in the story that tell about the characters. They will write and draw pictures on the construction paper to show what they find.

5. When groups have finished, have students go back to their original groups. Each detective is the group expert for the story element he or she investigated. Have them share clues and information.

6. Based on shared information, have groups put together a story retelling. Let them choose from these options: perform a skit, make a comic book, design a series of dioramas, write and illustrate a new version of the book, make a storyboard, perform a puppet show, or make a story map showing the sequence of events.

Story Sleuths Page 77

Ideas for More Differentiation

Have high-degree mastery students change one element of the story, such as the setting, and write a new version of the book. Have beginning mastery students focus on one element instead of all four. For example, let them work in groups to do a character study.

Extend the Activity

Have students work with Venn diagrams to compare story elements from two different books, such as two multicultural versions of a familiar fairy tale. For example, students could compare *Cendrillon: A Caribbean Cinderella* by Robert D. San Souci and *The Golden Sandal: A Middle Eastern Cinderella* by Rebecca Hickox.

Name _____ Date _____

Story Sleuths

Directions: Cut out the boxes. Pick a story element. Find out as much as you can about your story element.

Characters Who is the story about? 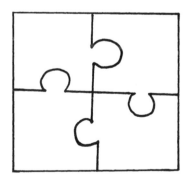	**Setting** Where does the story take place? 
Resolution How are all of the problems solved? 	**Problem** What problems happen in the story? 

In the Spotlight

Strategies

Graphic organizer

Multiple intelligences

Standard

Employ a wide range of writing strategies, and use different writing process elements appropriately to communicate with different audiences for a variety of purposes.

Objective

Students will select a focus for writing and use sensory details to describe an event.

Materials

Spotlight Idea Web reproducible
flashlight

Young students are often overwhelmed by writing assignments. They do not know what to write about or where to begin. In this activity, students use some prewriting techniques to develop a clear focus for a writing topic. Then they use a graphic organizer to help them brainstorm sensory details about their topic.

1. Help students get focused for this activity with a quick demonstration. Ask them to describe your classroom. After several descriptions, shine a flashlight on one object, and ask students to only describe that one thing. Explain that they will choose an event to put "in the spotlight."

2. Initiate a group discussion about things your students like to do and events they have attended. Record students' ideas on the board or a sheet of chart paper.

3. Choose a few items from the list, and ask volunteers to name three things they know about each one. Record those ideas, as well.

4. Then have each student list the names of three events he or she has attended. Encourage students to choose events that they know at least three things about. Have them circle one event, draw a picture of it, and independently brainstorm things they know about the event.

5. Next, give students a copy of the **Spotlight Idea Web reproducible (page 80)**. Have them use the graphic organizer to categorize their ideas. Encourage students to write down more ideas about their events using the five senses as inspiration. Ask them to think about what they saw, felt, heard, tasted, and touched.

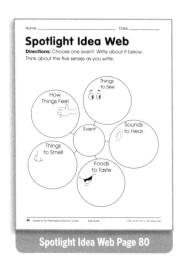

Spotlight Idea Web Page 80

6. Finally, have students write a short paragraph about the event they chose. Have them incorporate as many sensory details as they can. Allow volunteers to read their paragraphs aloud.

Ideas for More Differentiation

Allow beginning mastery writers to work with partners to write their stories. High-degree mastery writers may wish to write a chapter book about an event. Each chapter can feature a paragraph that focuses on one of the five senses.

Extend the Activity

Choose an event that all of your students have experienced, such as the first day of school. Make a class book about the event, and have each student contribute illustrations and a story or poem. Allow each student a chance to take the book home to share with their families. Then invite family members to add a story or poem of their own to the book. Your students will find the stories of each other's families fascinating!

Name _____ Date _____

Spotlight Idea Web

Directions: Choose one event. Write about it below.
Think about the five senses as you write.

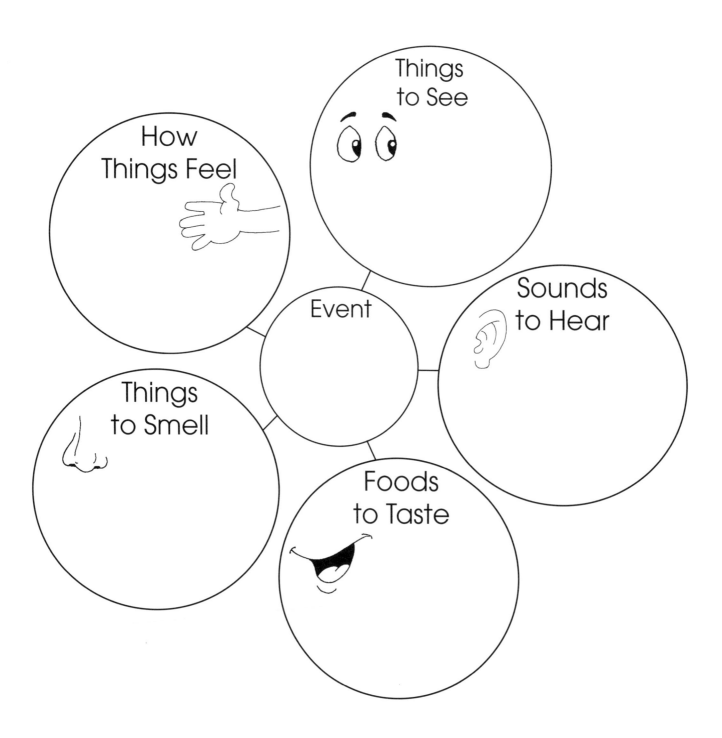

Funny Farm

Standard

Apply knowledge of language structure, language conventions (e.g., spelling and punctuation), media techniques, figurative language, and genre to create, critique, and discuss print and nonprint texts.

Objectives

Students will write sentences that accurately describe pictures.
Students will identify and correctly use singular nouns and plural nouns.

Materials

Funny Farm reproducible
construction paper
stapler
glue
scissors
crayons or markers

Strategy
Rehearsal

In this activity, students make minibooks that give them the opportunity to practice using singular and plural nouns. At the end of the activity, you will have a collection of books for students to share and enjoy together.

1. Review sentence structure with students. Explain that each sentence should begin with a capital letter and end with a period, question mark, or exclamation point.

2. Then review the rules for changing singular nouns to plural nouns. Write a list of nouns on the board, and have volunteers add –s or –es to make plurals. More advanced students may be able to work with words that end in –y and need the ending –ies to make plurals.

3. Fold three sheets of construction paper in half for each student, and staple them together to make minibooks.

4. Give students a copy of the **Funny Farm reproducible (page 83)**. Have them color the pictures and cut out the squares. Then have them glue the pictures to the pages in their minibooks. For the last two pages, have them draw their own "funny farm" pictures to write about (e.g., four cats playing tag or three sheep in a boat).

5. Have students write or dictate sentences to describe each picture. Then ask them to write a new sentence for each picture by

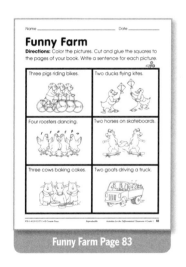

Funny Farm Page 83

changing the plural nouns to singular nouns. Have them draw pictures to go with the new sentences. Invite students to title their books and decorate the covers.

6. When the books are completed, invite each student to read several of his or her sentences aloud. Collect the books, and place them in your classroom library. Allow students to read the books independently. They can also read their books in pairs to compare their drawings, sentences, and plural nouns.

Ideas for More Differentiation

Let beginning mastery writers make double-sided flashcards to practice working with plural nouns. Have them write a singular noun on one side of the flashcard and its plural form on the opposite side. Have high-degree mastery writers use the pictures on the reproducible as story starters. Encourage them to write stories to describe the scenes.

Extend the Activity

For a simple sponge activity, say a sentence aloud that contains all singular nouns. Then ask a volunteer to change the sentence so it contains all plural nouns.

Funny Farm

Directions: Color the pictures. Cut and glue the squares to the pages of your book. Write a sentence for each picture.

Three pigs riding bikes. 	Two ducks flying kites. 
Four roosters dancing. 	Two horses on skateboards. 
Three cows baking cakes. 	Two goats driving a truck. 

CHAPTER 5

Physical Education, Art, and Music

Dance Party

Strategies

Multiple intelligences

Cooperative group learning

Objective

Students will combine three movements of their choice to create a simple dance routine and make a visual representation of their dance using symbols.

Materials

butcher paper
masking tape
crayons or markers
picture books about dance (see Book List)

Book List

Inspire your students to rumba, waltz, and swing as you read aloud books about dance. Here are some suggestions:

Barn Dance! by Bill Martin Jr. and John Archambault
Dinosaurumpus! by Tony Mitton
Frank Was a Monster Who Wanted to Dance by Keith Graves
Song and Dance Man by Karen Ackerman

This activity allows students with a wide variety of learning styles to feel successful. Bodily/kinesthetic learners and musical/rhythmic learners take center stage while choreographing a dance routine. Logical/mathematic learners and visual/spatial learners shine while diagramming the routine on a dance map. Finally, students with strong interpersonal skills appreciate the opportunity to work in groups.

1. Read aloud a picture book that features dancing characters. Select a book from the list provided, or choose another one you enjoy.

2. Have students identify some of the dance moves used in the book. These might include any of the following: *stand, walk, run, jump, slide, twist, lunge, stomp, spin, kick,* and *shake*. List the words on the board.

3. Tell students that people who plan, or choreograph, dances often create a dance map to record the movements. Review that a map is a picture that uses symbols to show where things are. In the

case of a dance map, symbols are used to show the sequence of movements that dancers will follow.

4. Have students suggest symbols for the words you listed on the board in Step 2. Draw the symbols next to the words.

5. Divide the class into small groups. Have each group create a simple dance routine that uses at least three of the movements listed on the board.

6. Give groups time to practice their routines. When they are satisfied with their dances, tape a length of butcher paper to the floor in front of each group. Let them use the dance symbols the class created together to draw a dance map for their routine.

7. Finally, allow each group to perform their dance for the class. Encourage the class to clap and give positive feedback to the dancers. Invite students to vote for the dance they like best.

Ideas for More Differentiation

Let more advanced students use simple classroom instruments like clappers and rhythm sticks to create simple songs or rhythms to accompany the dances. Let students who are not as comfortable with dance write poems to inspire the dance routines.

Extend the Activity

Take your dance show on the road! Have students visit other classes during physical education periods to teach their dance routines.

STAND TWIRL JUMP

Having a Ball with Balls

Strategies

Cooperative group learning

Center activities

Objective

Students will throw, catch, and kick balls with accuracy.

Materials

plywood sheet with holes cut out of it
playground balls of various sizes
beanbags
sidewalk chalk
limbo pole
handball wall

In this activity, students have a variety of opportunities to develop and improve their eye-hand and eye-foot coordination. Through a series of centers, they practice throwing, catching, and kicking balls and other objects. As students progress through the centers, their ability to accurately position the balls within a given area should improve. Divide students into small groups, and have the groups rotate through the following centers:

Center 1: Target Practice

Use a pencil to draw several different-sized circles on a sheet of plywood, and cut out the circles. The holes should be large enough for a beanbag to pass through. Hang the plywood or prop it up against a couple of chairs so it won't fall over easily. Have students take turns throwing beanbags at the targets. The goal is to throw the beanbags through the holes. You can choose to give holes point values (i.e., larger holes—fewer points; smaller holes—more points).

Center 2: Limbo Toss

Draw a large rectangle on the playground to identify the boundaries for this game. Set up a limbo pole in the center of the rectangle. Place the pole at the highest point. Divide the class into two groups, and have each group stand inside the boundaries on opposite sides of the limbo pole. Give one student a ball, and have him or her throw the ball to the other side of the play area. The ball must pass under the limbo pole. Another student catches the ball and then throws it back. When each student has had a turn throwing the ball under the pole, the pole is then lowered to the next level. Play continues until the pole is moved to the lowest level possible. As a variation, you can have students kick the ball rather than throw it.

978-1-4129-5337-5

Center 3: Wall Ball

Tell students to line up near a handball wall. Two students enter the play area together. Have one student kick a ball against the wall and the other student catch it. The catcher then kicks the ball, and the other student catches it. Let the pair continue playing until each one has kicked the ball five times. Then the next two players take a turn. As a variation, you can have students throw the ball rather than kick it.

Center 4: Pass the Ball

Establish a starting line and a finish line on a grass field. Students line up in two equal lines. Have the first two students in line run to the finish line while kicking a ball back and forth between them. On the return, they use a "chest pass" motion to throw the ball back and forth. Then the next two students in line take a turn.

Ideas for More Differentiation

You may wish to group students for these centers based on ability levels. More athletic students can work on developing speed and accuracy, while the less athletic students work on emerging skills.

Extend the Activity

Challenge student groups to create their own game that involves throwing and kicking. Have them teach the games to other groups.

Rub-a-Dub-Dub

Strategy
Center activity

Objective
Students will explore texture in art by making rubbings of various objects.

Materials
collection of art prints
objects with hard, uneven textures (leaves, sticks, rocks, wood, bark, bricks, feathers, blocks, coins)
drawing paper
unwrapped crayons
construction paper
scissors
glue

In this activity, students learn about how texture is used in art. First, they collect a variety of objects to use for rubbings. They then cut out the rubbings and arrange them to make a creative collage.

1. Prepare students for this activity by asking them to name objects that are hard, smooth, bumpy, scratchy, soft, silky, and so on. Tell them that all of these words tell about an object's texture, or how it feels. Explain that artists use texture in their work to show how things feel or how they might feel if they were touched. Display a variety of art prints, and ask students to describe the textures.

2. Tell students that they will make a collage using textures. Take students outside, and invite them to gather objects with texture (e.g., leaves, rocks, sticks, bark). When you return to the classroom, have students add to their collections anything you've already gathered.

3. Give students drawing paper and unwrapped crayons. Show them how to place the paper over an object and use the side of a crayon to rub over the top. Instruct students to rub lightly at first and then to press a little harder if they want a darker color.

4. Have each student do about ten rubbings. Then have them choose the ones they like best and cut them out. Let students arrange the rubbings on sheets of construction paper. Encourage students to experiment with different arrangements and with overlapping some of the shapes. When they are satisfied with their arrangements, they may glue the pieces in place.

5. Display students' finished artwork around the room. Invite the class to describe the textures shown in each piece.

Ideas for More Differentiation

Some students may wish to experiment with the use of color in their arrangements. If so, have them select the color of construction paper they want to use before doing the rubbings. Then students can decide if they want to use complementary colors, analogous colors, or monochromatic colors for their collages. Use a color wheel to help students visualize their color combinations before proceeding.

Extend the Activity

Let students experiment with adding texture to three-dimensional objects. Have them roll clay into balls and then use sticks to draw lines or poke holes into the clay. They can also add objects such as leaves and feathers to the clay balls.

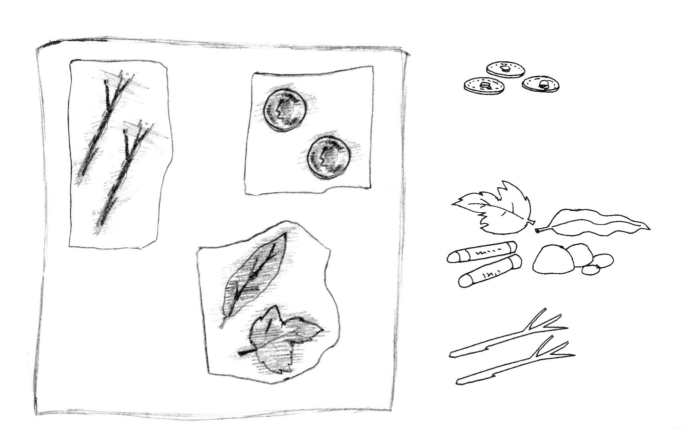

A World of Art

Strategies

Project

Cooperative group learning

Objective
Students will identify works of art from their own cultural backgrounds and compare art objects from various cultures.

Materials
A World of Art reproducible
world map
photo of each student
pushpins
yarn
reference materials about art from around the world

In this activity, students explore the richness of artwork from around the world. Students work with their families to learn about their personal cultural heritage and then work in groups to present artwork from those cultures.

1. Hang a world map on the bulletin board near the art center. Help students identify the continents and some of the countries. Pay special attention to countries that represent the cultural makeup of your class.

2. Use reference books or Web sites to show students pictures of artwork from around the world. Point out that art can take many forms—paintings, sculptures, fabrics, furniture, architecture, jewelry, and so on.

A World of Art Page 92

3. Assign the **A World of Art reproducible (page 92)** as a family homework project. When the homework is turned in, use the information gathered by families to help you design the rest of the lesson.

4. Staple students' photographs to the bulletin board with the world map. Use pushpins and yarn to connect the photographs to the countries from where students or their ancestors came. Be sure to honor each student's total cultural heritage by identifying all of the countries to which he or she has ancestral ties.

5. Explore the world map with students. Name the countries from where students or their ancestors came. Divide the class into small groups. Assign each group one of the countries identified on the map.

6. Have groups use the Internet, library books, encyclopedias, and other reference materials to locate examples of artwork from their

assigned countries. Depending on students' ability levels, you may have them find examples from several different categories of art, such as painting, sculpture, architecture, jewelry, and textiles.

7. Have each group give a brief presentation about the art samples they found. If possible, have them attach photocopies of their samples to the bulletin board. Help them use pushpins and yarn to connect the pictures to the countries on the world map.

Ideas for More Differentiation

Have students continue their investigations into different forms of art from around the world. Let artistically advanced students create reproductions of art objects in which they are interested. Students who are less confident in their artistic skills can create a collage using photographs of art objects found on the Internet.

Extend the Activity

Have students study the food, traditional dress, celebrations, and activities from cultures they learned about.

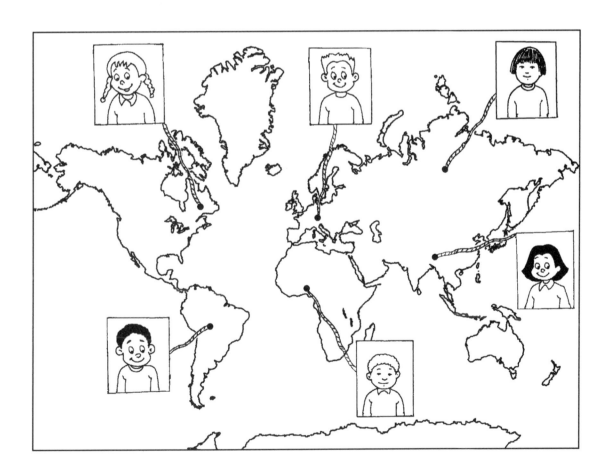

A World of Art

Directions: Have your family help you answer these questions.

1. From what countries are your ancestors?

_____

_ _

_____

2. What kind of art comes from this country?

_____

_ _

_____

3. Name an artist from that country. For what is he or she best known?

_____

_ _

_____

4. Draw a picture of artwork from this country.

Peter and the Wolf

Objective
Students will identify different musical instruments while listening to a recording of Prokofiev's *Peter and the Wolf.*

Strategies
Multiple intelligences

Cooperative group learning

Materials
Peter and the Wolf reproducible
recording of Sergei Prokofiev's *Peter and the Wolf*
photos of instruments (flute, oboe, clarinet, bassoon,
French horn, timpani drum, violin, viola, cello, double bass)
classroom instruments (recorders, bells, maracas,
triangles, rhythm sticks)
collection of familiar folktales
crayons or markers
craft sticks
scissors
glue

   Peter and the Wolf, written in 1936 by Sergei Prokofiev, is an excellent composition to use to teach students about the instruments and sounds of an orchestra. Students listen to a recording of the composition and practice identifying the instruments used to represent the characters. They then work in groups to retell familiar folktales using simple instruments to represent the characters.

1. Display the photos of the musical instruments. Ask students to identify as many of the instruments as they can. Tell them the names of the rest.

2. Use your computer to find a Web site about the composition *Peter and the Wolf*. Many Web sites offer short samples of the musical themes assigned to each character in the story. Try Phil Tulga: Music Through the Curriculm at: *www.philtulga.com/Peter.html*. Preview the site before introducing it to students. Then play the music samples to show students what each instrument sounds like on its own.

3. Give students a copy of the **Peter and the Wolf reproducible (page 95)**. Have them color and cut out the pictures of the instruments and glue each one to a craft stick.

4. Play the complete recording of *Peter and the Wolf*. As students are listening, ask them to identify the instruments they hear by holding up the pictures they glued to craft sticks.

Peter and the Wolf Page 95

5. Discuss with students how the music and the words work together to tell the story.

6. Divide the class into small groups. Let each group choose a folktale with which they are familiar and use classroom instruments to develop a short musical cue to identify each character in the folktale. Give groups ample time to practice before presenting their readings to the class.

7. Invite each group to present their folktale and musical accompaniment to the class. Advanced readers can read aloud, while those with musical skills can supply the background music.

Ideas for More Differentiation

Encourage high-degree mastery students to work in groups to write their own simple folktales with musical accompaniment.

Extend the Activity

Invite community musicians to visit your classroom and perform songs for students.

Peter and the Wolf

Directions: Color and cut out the pictures. Glue them to sticks.

Flute

Oboe

Clarinet

Bassoon

French Horn

Timpani

String Instruments

References

California Department of Education. (2005). *History–social science framework for California public schools: Kindergarten through grade 12.* Sacramento, CA: California Department of Education.

California Department of Education. (2006). *Mathematics framework for California public schools: Kindergarten through grade 12.* Sacramento, CA: California Department of Education.

California Department of Education. (1994). *Physical education framework for California public schools: Kindergarten through grade 12.* Sacramento, CA: California Department of Education.

California Department of Education. (1999). *Reading/language arts framework for California public schools: Kindergarten through grade 12.* Sacramento, CA: California Department of Education.

California Department of Education. (2004). *Science framework for California public schools: Kindergarten through grade 12.* Sacramento, CA: California Department of Education.

California Department of Education. (2004). *Visual and performing arts framework for California public schools: Kindergarten through grade 12.* Sacramento, CA: California Department of Education.

Create a graph. (n.d.). Retrieved September 15, 2006, from the Kids Zone Learning with NCES Web site: http://nces.ed.gov/nceskids/createagraph.

Federal holidays. (n.d.). Retrieved September 30, 2006, from the U.S. Office of Personnel Management Web site: http://www.opm.gov/fedhol.

Gregory, G. H., & Chapman, C. (2002). *Differentiated instructional strategies: One size doesn't fit all, second edition.* Thousand Oaks, CA: Corwin Press.

Local weather. (n.d.). Retrieved September 15, 2006, from the Weather Channel Web site: http://www.weather.com.

National Council for the Social Studies. (2002). *Expectations of excellence: Curriculum standards for social studies.* Silver Spring, MD: National Council for the Social Studies (NCSS).

National Council of Teachers of English and International Reading Association. (1996). *Standards for the English language arts.* Urbana, IL: National Council of Teachers of English (NCTE).

National Council of Teachers of Mathematics. (2005). *Principles and standards for school mathematics.* Reston, VA: National Council of Teachers of Mathematics (NCTM).

National Research Council. (2005). *National science education standards.* Washington, DC: National Academy Press.

Rosenberg, M. (2006). *The 193 countries on earth with their capital city or cities.* Retrieved September 15, 2006, from the About: Geography Web site: http://geography.about.com/od/countryinformation/a/capitals.htm.

Tulga, P. (2006). *Peter and the wolf: A musical story by Sergei Prokofiev.* Retrieved October 1, 2006, from the Phil Tulga: Music Through the Curriculum Web site: http://philtulga.com/Peter.html.